PILOT'S FLIGHT OPERATING INSTRUCTIONS

FOR

ARMY MODELS

P-38H Series, P-38J Series, P-38L-1 L-5 and F-5B AIRPLANES

This publication contains specific instructions for pilots and should be available for Transition Flying Training as contemplated in AAF Reg. 50-16.

Appendix I of this publication shall not be carried in aircraft on combat missions or when there is a reasonable chance of its falling into the hands of the enemy.

Published under joint authority of the Commanding General, Army Air Forces, the Chief of the Bureau of Aeronautics, and the Air Council of the United Kingdom.

NOTICE: This document contains information affecting the national defense of the United States within the meaning of the Espionage Act, 50 U. S. C., 31 and 32, as amended. Its transmission or the revelation of its contents in any manner to an unauthorized person is prohibited by law.

ISBN No. 0-87994-019-0

FOREWORD

At this writing, more than a quarter of a century after the cessation of hostilities of World War Two, the Lockheed P—38 Lightning , will bring back several different types of memories depending on the generation of the reader. To the under—30 group, most likely the only contact is old Van Johnson — June Allison movies seen on late night TV. To the over—40 group memories of the courage and heroism of Major Richard Bong will be conjured up. The over—50 aviation enthusiast will vividly recall the names of such places as The Bulge, Salerno, Anzio Beach, Ploesti, Leyte Gulf, Guadalcanal, Okinawa, all places where the P—38 served with distinction.

In reality, most aircraft are made up of an evolutionary process of constant develop—ment and improvement, and the Lightning is no exception. The design concept had its origin in 1936 and the first XP—38 flew on 27 January, 1939. A few weeks later this model crashed on landing, but the design proved to be sufficiently sound to prompt the U.S. Government to contract for the manufacture of 673 airplanes of this design. These first ones ordered utilized Allison engines.

In the summer of 1941, with hostilities in Europe accelerating daily, thirty production models were delivered by Lockheed. The evolutionary process continued with 210 of Model P—38 E and 527 of Model P—38 F the first model with torpedo or 1000 lb. bomb capacity. This was quickly followed by an order for 1082 of Model P—38 G and 601 of Model P—38 H, which now used the 1425 Hp. Allison engines and capable of carrying two 1600 lb. bombs. By this time the American industrial strength had been converted into a war economy, supplying its own needs and providing Lend Lease aircraft to England and the Soviet Union. The three models covered by this manual were produced in the largest quantities for immediate deployment: 2970 P—38 J, 3923 P—38 L, and the final model was the two—man radar equipped P—38 M, which saw considerable action in the Pacific Theatre as a night fighter. As the war progressed more than one thousand of the later models (J & L) were converted to use as photo reconnaisance craft. This new function ideally suited the P—38 with its high speed of 414 mph. and service ceiling of 44,000 feet and effective maximum range of almost 2300 miles. The total wartime pro—duction of all models of the Lockheed Lightning is an impressive 9,923 units.

The first recorded combat action and victory for the P—38 was in August of 1942 when a German Focke—Wulf Kurier was shot down over the North Atlantic. A total of some 2500 victories were credited to the Lightning in the European Campaign, with losses of 1750. One of the most daring exploits of the war occured on 10 June, 1944 when the P—38's were assigned to destroy the German—held Ploesti oil fields and refineries in Roumania. The mission flew along the Danube River at tree top level as far as Budapest, then by sharply changing course flew directly to Ploesti, where the mission was completely successful in destroying the cracking towers of the refinery. This mission ended the dreams of the Luftwaffe forever.

Due to the unusual silhouette of the P—38 and its high speed it was employed as the aircraft cover for the Normandy Invasion. It was felt that with the large number of very inexperienced gunners aboard the invasion fleet the airplane least likely to be confused with the Luftwaffe's aircraft, would be the Lightning. D-Day was also the most disastrous day for the P—38; twenty—three planes and an equal number of men were lost.

One of the serious drawbacks of the Lightning which led to its gradual elimination as a combat plane was the high cost of maintenance. It was found that the single— engined fighters such as the P—40 , P—47 , P—51 , and the fantastically effective British Spitfire could be operated for one—half the cost of the P—38. This observation pretty well doomed the twin engine fighter.

Late in the war some of the P—38's were pressed into service by the Free French, the Italian Aerobrigata, the Chinese Nationalist Air Force. After the hostilities ended the Lightning quickly fell out of vogue. Most were sold for scrap, a few given to the allies for use as trainers, some were used for racing, a few went to oil companies for aerial surveying, and to this day a very few can be seen at air shows. Fortunately some have survived in Museums.

Description

1. AIRPLANE.

a. GENERAL.

(1) The P-38H, P-38J, P-38L, and F-5B airplanes are twin boomed, single place monoplanes manufactured by the Lockheed Aircraft Corporation. P-38H, P-38J, and P-38L are fighter airplanes. The F-5B is a photographic airplane. Hydraulically operated landing gear, flaps, brakes, and coolant shutters are provided. (Late airplanes are equipped with hydraulically boosted aileron control.) The approximate overall dimensions are as follows:

Length	37 feet 10 inches
Height (top of prop rad.)	12 feet 10 inches
Span	52 feet 0 inches

(2) The armament is mounted in the nose of the fuselage, and armor protection is provided as shown in figure 2. Photographic airplanes are protected by armor the same as the fighters, but all armament is replaced by cameras.

b. FLIGHT CONTROLS.

(1) TRIM TABS.—Trim tabs are mounted on all the movable surfaces and are controllable from the cockpit during flight. Airplanes equipped with aileron control booster do not have aileron trim tabs.

(2) FLAPS.—The flaps are a Lockheed modified Fowler type.

(a) CONTROLS.—Flap action is controlled by the lever (figure 7-2) on the right-hand side of the cockpit. When the lever is placed to UP, DOWN, or MANEUVER, the flaps will automatically stop at the desired position. The lever should be returned to CLOSED as soon as the end position is reached. The control will not go to the DOWN position until the trigger on the lever is lifted through the notch just forward of the CLOSED position.

Note

When using maneuvering flaps, the flap lever must be left in the MANEUVER position. If it is moved even slightly forward and then returned to MANEUVER, the flaps will extend completely. (This condition is corrected on late airplanes.)

(b) POSITION INDICATOR. — On the early airplanes, flap position is indicated by the flap and landing gear position indicator on the instrument panel. On late airplanes the flap position is indicated by a small pop-up lever (figure 3) on the trailing edge of the left center section just inside the boom. This indicator projects above the wing whenever the flaps are not full up.

(3) SURFACE CONTROL LOCK. — The surface control lock (figure 7-10) is stowed on the right-hand window sill and extends across the center of the cockpit when in use. On the late airplanes this lock does not lock the rudders.

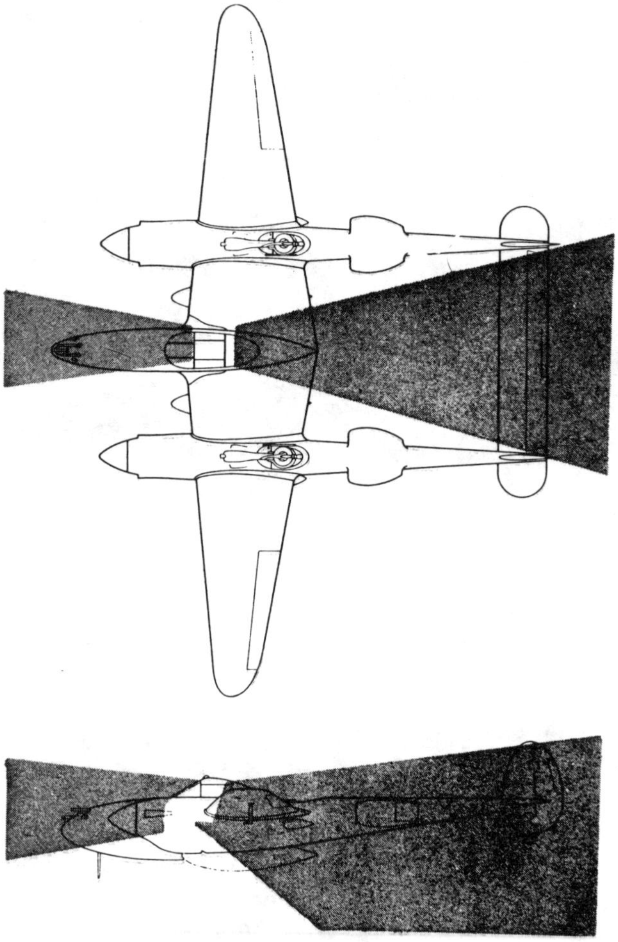

these airplanes most of the aileron control force is provided by hydraulic boost; the remainder is applied by the pilot. Figure 15 illustrates the control linkage. Control cables which control the boost mechanism are mechanically connected to the control surfaces, allowing manual flight control in an emergency. The aileron boost shut-off valve (figure 9-5), is located on the right side of the cockpit near the pilot's control column. In addition to this valve an automatic by-pass valve is incorporated in the mechanism to allow free movement of the ailerons in case the hydraulic pressure should fail.

IMPORTANT

The ailerons ride approximately one inch higher with boost OFF. This change in trim is normal.

c. LANDING GEAR. *(See figure 16.)*

(1) The landing gear lever (figures 4-32) controls the extension and retraction of all three wheels. A lock on the lever prevents the lever from being moved out of the DOWN position when the airplane is on the ground (when the left main shock strut is compressed). If this lock fails, or if it is necessary to retract the landing gear on the ground because of engine failure at take-off, the lock may be released by rotating the landing gear control release-knob (figure 4-33) in a counterclockwise direction.

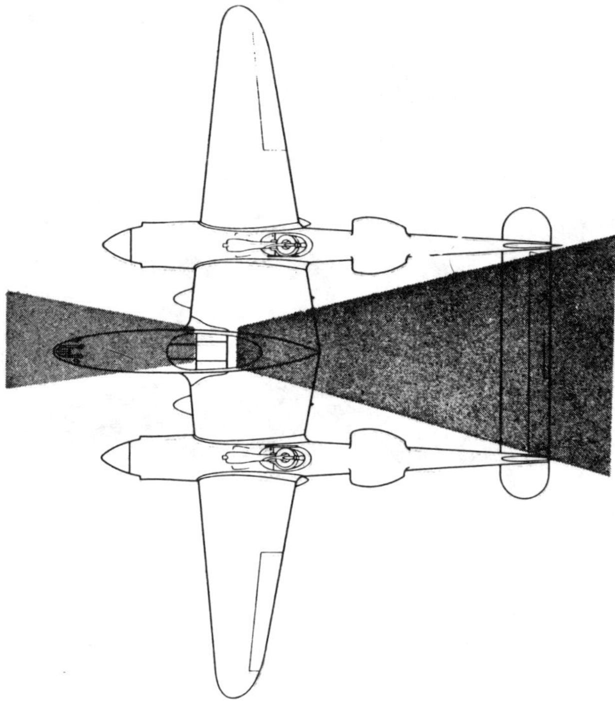

Figure 2 — Armor Protection

(4) AUTOMATIC PILOT.—A type A-4 automatic pilot is installed in the F-5B airplane. The automatic pilot control unit is on the instrument panel; the shut-off valve (figure 24-10) is below the instrument panel; and the automatic pilot oil pressure gage (figure 33-10) is on the center control stand.

(5) DIVE RECOVERY FLAP. — P-38L and late P-38J airplanes are equipped with electrically operated dive recovery flaps which are controlled by a switch (figure 9-2) on the pilot's control wheel. The dive recovery flaps will extend or retract within two seconds.

(6) AILERON CONTROL HYDRAULIC BOOSTER. — P-38L and late P-38J airplanes are equipped with hydraulically boosted aileron control. On

Figure 3 — Flap Pop-up Indicator

1. Spotlight (normal position).
2. Throttles.
3. Surface controls lock clip.
4. Propeller controls.
5. Propeller selector switches.
6. Mixture controls.
7. Propeller warning lights (P-38H only).
8. Carburetor air filter control. (Late airplanes.) (Control not used on early airplanes.)
9. Propeller circuit breaker buttons.
10. Gun charger handle (on early airplanes only).
11. Ignition switches.
12. Cannon trigger button. (Machine gun button on forward side of wheel.) (Switch arrangements vary with different airplane models.)
13. Propeller feathering switches.
14. Parking brake handle.
15. Microphone button. (Location varies with airplane model.)
16. Gun charging selector knob (P-38H only).
17. Landing gear warning light. (Early airplanes only.)
18. Propeller lever vernier knob.
19. Friction control.
20. Bomb or tank release selector switches.
21. Bomb or tank release indicator lights.
22. Cockpit light.
23. Gun (or camera) compartment heat control. (Cockpit heat on later airplanes.)
24. Arm-safe switch. (Bombs.)
25. Arming indicator light.
26. Safe indicator light.
27. Bomb or droppable tank release button.
28. Spare indicator lights.
29. Spotlight alternate position socket.
30. Cockpit ventilator control.
31. Gun sight dark glass stowage. (Early airplanes only.)
32. Landing gear control handle.
33. Landing gear control release.
34. Oxygen pressure gage.
35. Elevator tab control.
36. Engine primer.

Figure 4 — Cockpit — Left-hand Side

(2) POSITION INDICATOR.

On P-38H, early P-38J and F-5B airplanes, the landing gear position is indicated on the instrument panel by the flap and landing gear position indicator. A light on the control stand, and a warning horn operate when either throttle is closed if the landing gear is not locked down. On later P-38J and F-5B, and all P-38L airplanes, the position indicator and warning light on the engine control stand have been replaced by a warning light (figure 8-24) on the instrument panel. The warning light glows whenever the landing gear is in transit - not locked up or down. With either throttle closed the warning light glows unless the landing gear is down and locked.

(3) BRAKES.—The brake system is not connected to the main hydraulic system. No emergency braking system is provided. See figure 18 for brake system diagram.

d. HYDRAULIC SYSTEM. *(See figures 14 and 16.)*

(1) Normal system pressure (figure 8-22) is between 1100 to 1400 psi, surge to 1600 psi permissible. See Section IV for emergency operating instructions.

(2) There are three separate systems of operation for the hydraulic equipment in this airplane.

(a) The normal system operates all the hydraulic equipment (except brakes) using hydraulic pressure from the engine driven hydraulic pumps and hydraulic fluid from the top half of the main hydraulic fluid reservoir.

(b) The auxiliary system operates the same equipment and uses the same lines as the normal system except that the hand hydraulic pump furnishes the hydraulic pressure and the fluid comes from the bottom of the main hydraulic fluid reservoir. When the auxiliary system is in use the hand pump source selector valve (figure 17-4) is UP and the bypass valve (figure 17-3) is OPEN.

Note

It will be impossible to build up pressure with the hand pump unless the aileron boost valve is OFF and the coolant override switches are OFF. The coolant override valves have a fixed bleed in the system when the switches are in the override position.

(c) The emergency system is used to extend the landing gear in case of complete failure of the normal and auxiliary systems. The emergency system is equipped with a separate reservoir and separate lines. Pressure is supplied by the hand pump. When the emergency system is in use the hand pump source selector valve is DOWN and the bypass valve is CLOSED. (Late airplanes have the bypass valve incorporated in the source selector valve.)

e. ELECTRICAL SYSTEM.

(1) GENERAL.—On P-38H and early P-38J airplanes, the 24 volt electrical system is powered by a generator on the left engine and by a battery. F-5B, P-38L, and late P-38J airplanes have a generator on each engine and a battery. On fighter airplanes the battery is in the left boom, and on photographic airplanes the battery is in the nose compartment. The battery switch (figure 5-15) cuts out the battery, leaving the rest of the system operating on the generator(s). The generator switch (figure 5-16) (two switches on late airplanes, figure 8-11) turns off the power from the generator, allowing the system to draw power from the battery only. The ignition master switch (figure 5-1) is not connected to the airplane's electrical system, and turns off the ignition only to both engines.

(2) CIRCUIT BREAKERS AND FUSES.—On late airplanes, circuit breakers are used to replace the fuses previously located in the nose gear wheel well. These circuit breakers are mounted along the right forward side of the cockpit (figure 6) and act as fuses to automatically break the circuit whenever an overload occurs. They may be reset by allowing a short interval for cooling and then pushing the button.

Note

It is not possible to tell by visual inspection whether or not a circuit breaker is open.

(3) LIGHTS.

(a) LANDING LIGHTS.—The landing light is located under the left wing and controlled by a switch (figure 5-7) on the main switch box. P-38H airplanes have a landing light under each wing, with individual switches. With the switch ON the light turns on and extends. On P-38H airplanes, when the switches are turned OFF the lights turn off, but remain extended. On F-5B and early P-38J airplanes when the switch is turned OFF the lights remain ON and extended. Later P-38J and P-38L airplanes have the landing light recessed in the left wing leading edge. The landing lights should not be used unnecessarily, as the life of the lamps is approximately 25 hours.

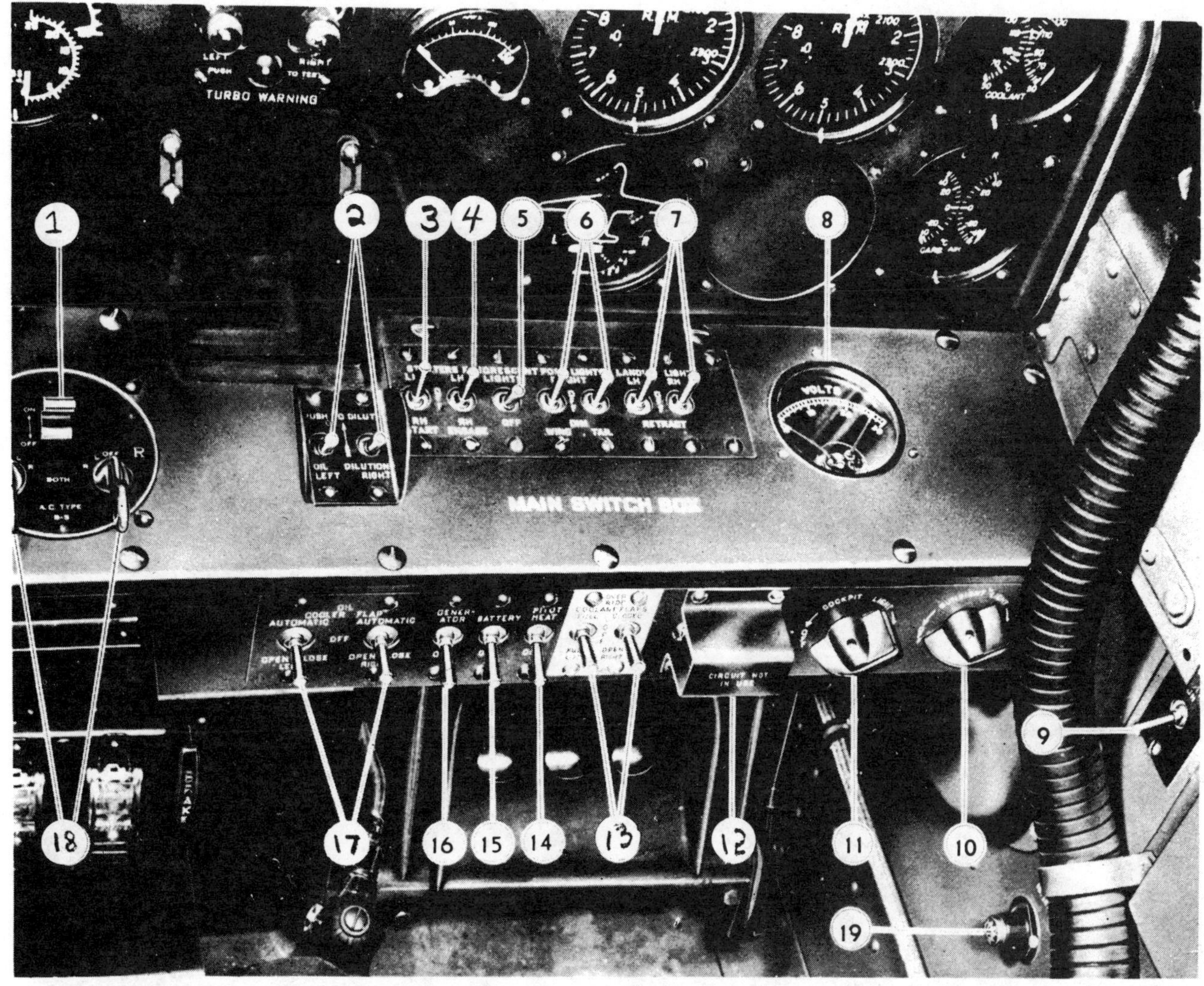

1. Ignition master switch.
2. Oil dilution switches
3. Starter switch.
4. Engage switch.
5. Flourescent light switch.
6. Position light switches.
7. Landing light switches (left-hand only on P-38J, P-38L, and F-5B).
8. Voltmeter.
9. Inverter switch (P-38H).
10. Gun sight light rheostat (on control column on later airplanes).
11. Cockpit light rheostat.
12. Intercooler flap switches. (P-38J, P-38L, and F-5B. Circuit not in use on P-38H.)
13. Coolant flap override switches.
14. Pitot heat switch.
15. Battery switch.
16. Generator switch.
17. Oil cooler flap switches.
18. Ignition switches.
19. Inverter warning light (P-38H).

Figure 5 — Main Switch Box

1. Fluorescent light rheostat (late airplanes).
2. Landing light.
3. Starter and booster.
4. Cross suction and oil dilution.
5. R.H. fuel pump.
6. L.H. fuel pump.
7. Cockpit lights.
8. Position lights.
9. Recognition lights.
10. Bomb and droppable tank release.
11. Camera and armament firing and solenoids and relays.
12. Camera and armament firing and solenoids and relays.
13. Contactor heater switch.

14. SCR-695 radio.
15. Range receiver.
16. SCR-274N and SCR-522A Receivers.
17. Radio dynamotor.
18. Fuel gages.
19. Temperature instruments.
20. Oxygen and landing gear warning.
21. Coolant override.
22. Right intercooler flap motor.
23. Left intercooler flap motor.
24. Right oil cooler flap motor.
25. Left oil cooler flap motor.

Figure 6 — Circuit Breakers

(b) RECOGNITION LIGHTS.—These airplanes have three downward lights, red, green, and amber. White lights are on some airplanes.

CAUTION

It is possible to burn the plastic lenses of the downward recognition lights by operating them for more than thirty seconds while on the ground.

(c) POSITION LIGHTS.—The position lights are controlled by switches (figure 5-6) on the main switch box.

(d) COCKPIT LIGHTS. *(Figures 7-12 and 4-22).* —These lights are controlled by a rheostat (figure 5-11) on the main switch box and by a switch on the lights themselves.

(e) FLUORESCENT INSTRUMENT LIGHTS. —The fluorescent lights are mounted on the forward side of the pilot's control column and are turned ON by a switch (figure 5-5) on the main switch box. Light intensity is regulated by twisting the ends of the lighting unit.

(f) SPOTLIGHT. *(Figure 4-1).*—The spotlight is normally on the left windshield support. An alternate position (figure 4-29) is provided over the fuel tank selector valves. The spotlight switch is located on the light. The beam may be focused by sliding the screw head forward and aft in its slot.

(4) INVERTER.—On P-38H airplanes the inverter is turned on by the switch (figure 5-9) under the flap control lever. It supplies alternating current to operate the fluorescent lights and the remote indicating compass. A warning light (figure 5-19) glows when the inverter is not operating, indicating failure of the inverter and consequent failure of the compass and fluorescent lights.

(a) On P-38J, P-38L, and F-5B airplanes the inverter operates only the compass and is turned on by a switch (labeled COMPASS) on the main switch box. No warning light is installed.

f. PILOT COMFORT.

(1) The rudder pedals are adjusted by pushing or pulling the small lever (figure 7-18) on the outboard corner of each pedal and moving the pedals to suit. Care must be taken to insure that both pedals are adjusted equally.

(2) The seat is adjusted by lifting the small lever (figure 17-1) on the right side of the seat and raising or lowering the seat as required. After the lever is released, check to make sure the seat is firmly locked in the new position.

(3) Shoulder harness should be worn at all times. It will be impossible to lean forward unless the harness lever (figure 13-7) on the left side of the pilot's seat is raised. The harness lock will re-engage as soon as an upright position is resumed.

(4) PILOT'S RELIEF TUBE. *(Figure 7-16.)*

2. POWER PLANT.

a. ENGINES.—P-38H, P-38J, and F-5B airplanes are powered by one V-1710-89 right-hand rotating engine and one V-1710-91 left-hand rotating engine. P-38L airplanes are powered by one V-1710-111 right-hand rotating engine and one V-1710-113 left-hand rotating engine. These are 12-cylinder V-type liquid-cooled Allison engines. The engines drive three-bladed, constant-speed, full-feathering Curtiss electric propellers.

b. FUEL, OIL, AND COOLANT SPECIFICATIONS.

Fuel.....Specification AN-7-28, Grade 100/130 or Specification AN-7-26, Grade 91.

Oil......Specification AN-VV-O-446, Grade 1120 (for cold weather operation, Grade 1100A).

Coolant..Specification AN-E-2 (Ethylene Glycol— Inhibited with NaMBT).

c. FUEL SYSTEM. *(See figures 10, 10A, and 11.)*

A separate fuel system is provided for each engine. Fuel may also be cross-fed to the opposite engine during single engine operation or when operating on the droppable tanks.

The booster pump switches and the tank selector valves are on the left beside the pilot's seat. On airplanes equipped with outer wing tanks, the outer wing tank low level warning lights are in the forward left-hand corner of the cockpit. On unmodified airplanes the engine priming pump is on the floor in front of the seat. On modified airplanes the priming-oil dilution switch is on the main switch box.

Note

All P-38L-5 airplanes and some P-38L-1 and P-38J airplanes are equipped with a modified fuel system. The new system may be readily identified by the two booster pump master switches (figure 13A-4) and the two speed control switches (figure 13A-3). All airplanes equipped with the old system will be referred to as unmodified airplanes and airplanes equipped with the new system will be referred to as modified airplanes.

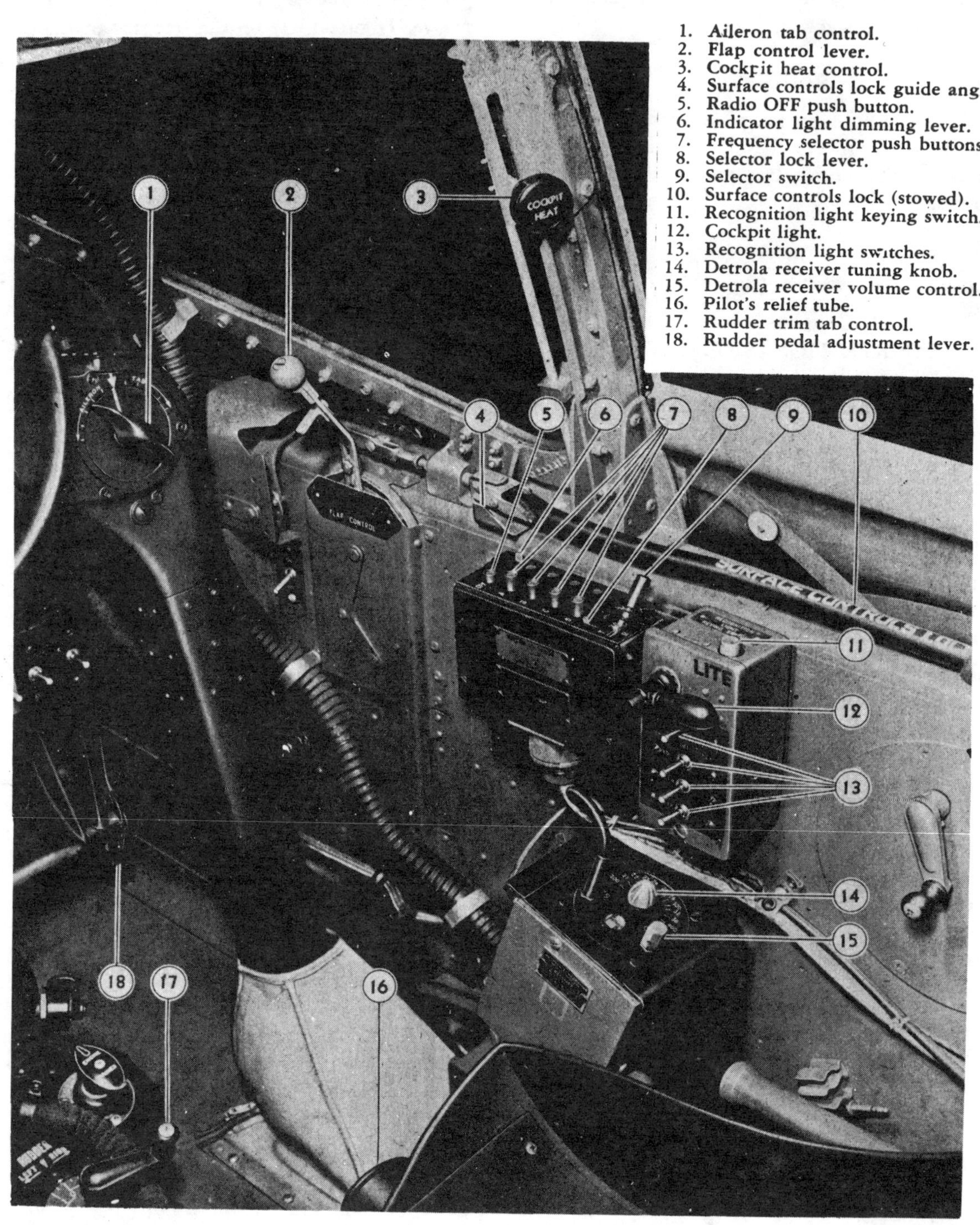

1. Aileron tab control.
2. Flap control lever.
3. Cockpit heat control.
4. Surface controls lock guide angle.
5. Radio OFF push button.
6. Indicator light dimming lever.
7. Frequency selector push buttons.
8. Selector lock lever.
9. Selector switch.
10. Surface controls lock (stowed).
11. Recognition light keying switch.
12. Cockpit light.
13. Recognition light switches.
14. Detrola receiver tuning knob.
15. Detrola receiver volume control.
16. Pilot's relief tube.
17. Rudder trim tab control.
18. Rudder pedal adjustment lever.

Figure 7 — Cockpit — Right-hand Side

1. Standby magnetic compass.
2. Suction gage.
3. Clock.
4. Gyro Horizon.
5. Manifold pressure gages (left and right).
6. Tachometers (left and right).
7. Engine gage right engine (oil temperature and pressure and fuel pressure).
8. Coolant temperature gage.
9. Carburetor air temperature gage.
10. BC-608 contactor.
11. Generator switches.
12. Ammeters.
13. Compass correction cards.
14. Engine gage left engine (oil temperature and pressure and fuel pressure).
15. Rate of climb indicator.
16. Bank and turn indicator.
17. Airspeed indicator.
18. Directional gyro.
19. Remote indicating compass.
20. Front (reserve) fuel tanks quantity gage.
21. Rear (main) fuel tanks quantity gage.
22. Hydraulic pressure gage.
23. Altimeter.
24. Landing gear warning light.
25. Landing gear warning light test button.
26. Spare bulb.

Figure 8 — Typical Instrument Panel (P-38J-25 Panel Shown)

1. Control wheel switches (cannon and machine gun trigger, bomb release, etc.).
2. Dive recovery flap control switch.
3. Microphone switch.
4. Propeller feathering switch warning lights.
5. Aileron boost shut-off valve (late airplanes).
6. Gun sight light rheostat (late airplanes).

Figure 9 — Control Wheel

d. OIL SYSTEM. *(See figure 19.)*

(1) OIL DILUTION.—The oil dilution system is controlled by two switches on the main switch box (figure 5-2).

(2) TEMPERATURE CONTROL.—Oil temperature control is automatic when the switches (figure 5-17) are set to automatic. In case of failure of the automatic system, manual control over the oil cooler flaps may be obtained by means of the same switches.

e. THROTTLE CONTROL.—The throttle is mechanically connected to the supercharger regulator so that control of the supercharger as a separate operation has been eliminated. Early airplanes are equipped with turbo-supercharger overspeed warning lights which flicker when rated turbo speed is reached and glow steadily when war emergency speed is reached. Late airplanes are equipped with turbo-supercharger regulators incorporating two overspeed controls. The normal overspeed control regulates to 24,000 turbo rpm. The War Emergency overspeed control regulates to 26,400 turbo rpm and comes into operation whenever the throttles are advanced past the take-off stops. The overspeed warning lights are deleted from these airplanes. These late airplanes are also equipped with manifold pressure regulators. With these two regulators, each manifold pressure has a corresponding cockpit throttle position which is fixed for all altitudes up to the critical altitude. (Critical altitude is the altitude where the overspeed governor takes control). Above critical altitude, the turbo rpm is held constant at either 24,000 or 26,400, depending on the throttle position, and the manifold pressure will automatically drop approximately 1½″ Hg. for every 1000 feet above critical altitude.

Thus above critical altitude, if it is desired to reduce the manifold pressure, no reduction will be obtained until the throttle is pulled back to the position which would normally give the manifold pressure then being allowed by the overspeed control. At manifold pressures below that being allowed, the power plant is operating below its critical altitude and throttle operation is normal. If it is desired to increase the manifold pressure, no change will occur until the throttle is past the take-off stop. At this point the War Emergency overspeed control comes into operation and the supercharger speed increases to 26,400 rpm with a corresponding rapid increase in manifold pressure. This increase is approximately 5″ Hg. and no intermediate settings can be made.

f. MIXTURE CONTROLS.—The mixture controls (figure 4-6) have four positions, FULL RICH, (Wired off in some planes) RICH, AUTO LEAN, and CUT-OFF.

g. PROPELLER CONTROLS.

(1) PROPELLER CONTROL LEVERS.— These levers (figure 4-4) select the desired engine rpm for automatic constant speed propeller operation.

(2) PROPELLER SELECTOR SWITCHES (*figure 4-5*). These switches have four positions:

(a) AUTO CONSTANT SPEED. — The propeller governors are in operation and engine speed will be maintained as set on the propeller levers.

(b) FIXED PITCH. — Propeller pitch is fixed, engine speed depends upon power and airplane speed.

(c) INC RPM.—Engine speed increases with lower pitch.

(d) DEC RPM.—Engine speed decreases with higher pitch.

(3) PROPELLER CIRCUIT BREAKERS.—These circuit breakers open, and the propeller pitch changing mechanism becomes inoperative, when the current required to operate the propellers becomes too high. When the circuit breakers open, the buttons (figure 4-9) pop up, disclosing a red and white band on the buttons. The circuit breakers may be reset by pushing the buttons after allowing approximately 15 seconds for the switches to cool. Only the black portion of the buttons is visible when the circuit breakers are properly set.

(4) FEATHERING SWITCHES. (*Figure 4-13.*)— These switches turn the propellers to their minimum drag position. Late airplanes are equipped with indicator lights which glow over the proper feathering switch when either a hard left or hard right rudder

control is applied to overcome the yaw caused by failure of one engine at low air speed.

(5) WARNING LIGHTS. (*Figure 4-7.*) — Propeller warning lights are installed on P-38H airplanes only. They indicate when the propeller circuits are not properly set for take-off and landing, that is, when the circuit breakers are open, or the selector switches are not set to AUTO CONSTANT SPEED. These lights, however, do not warn of an improperly set propeller control lever

(6) VERNIER KNOB. (*Figure 4-18.*)—The vernier knob provides for fine adjustment of the right-hand propeller pitch control when synchronizing the engines.

(7) FRICTION CONTROL. (*Figure 4-19.*)—The friction control may be adjusted to prevent the throttles and propeller controls from creeping out of their set position.

h. CARBURETOR AIR TEMPERATURE CONTROLS.

(1) P-38H airplanes are not provided with a control for the carburetor air temperature, as the intercoolers are located in the wings and there are no intercooler flaps. On P-38J, P-38L, and F-5B airplanes a core type intercooler is located under each engine, and the intercooler flap, controlling carburetor air temperature, is operated by the switches (figure 5-12) on the face of the main switch box.

i. CARBURETOR AIR FILTER CONTROL.

(1) This control is located behind the pilot's seat on early airplanes. On late airplanes, this control is located on the engine control stand (figure 4-8).

j. COOLANT TEMPERATURE CONTROLS.

(1) Coolant temperature is automatically regulated between 101°C (214°F) (flaps closed) and 121°C (250°F) (flaps open) with the coolant flap override switches set to OFF.

(2) The override switches (figure 5-13) may be operated to fully OPEN or fully CLOSE the flaps in the event that the regulators fail to maintain the above temperatures. It is not possible to set the coolant flaps to any position except full OPEN or full CLOSE when using the override switches. If hydraulic pressure fails completely, the flaps will assume a faired (mid) position.

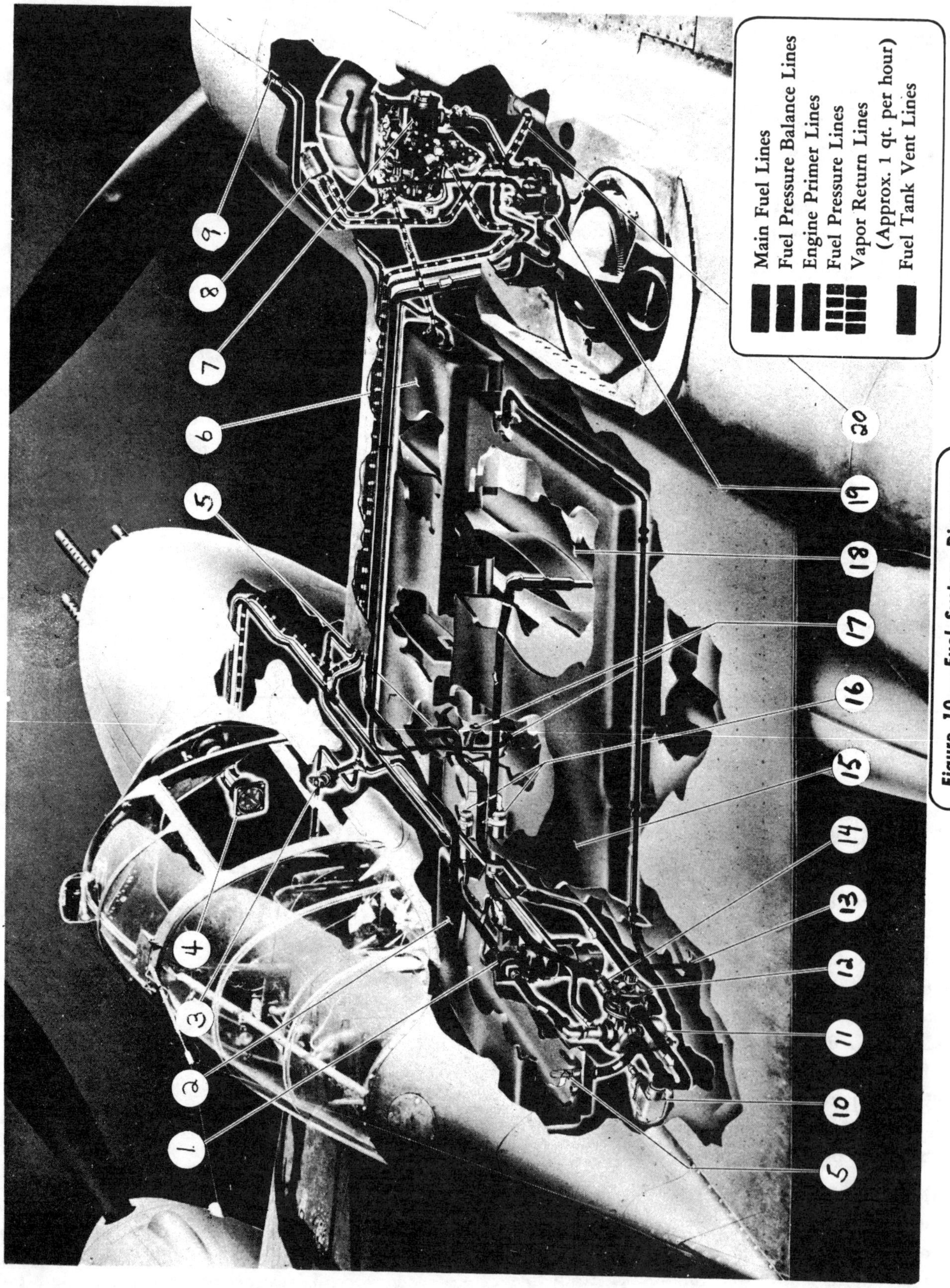

Figure 10 — Fuel System Diagram

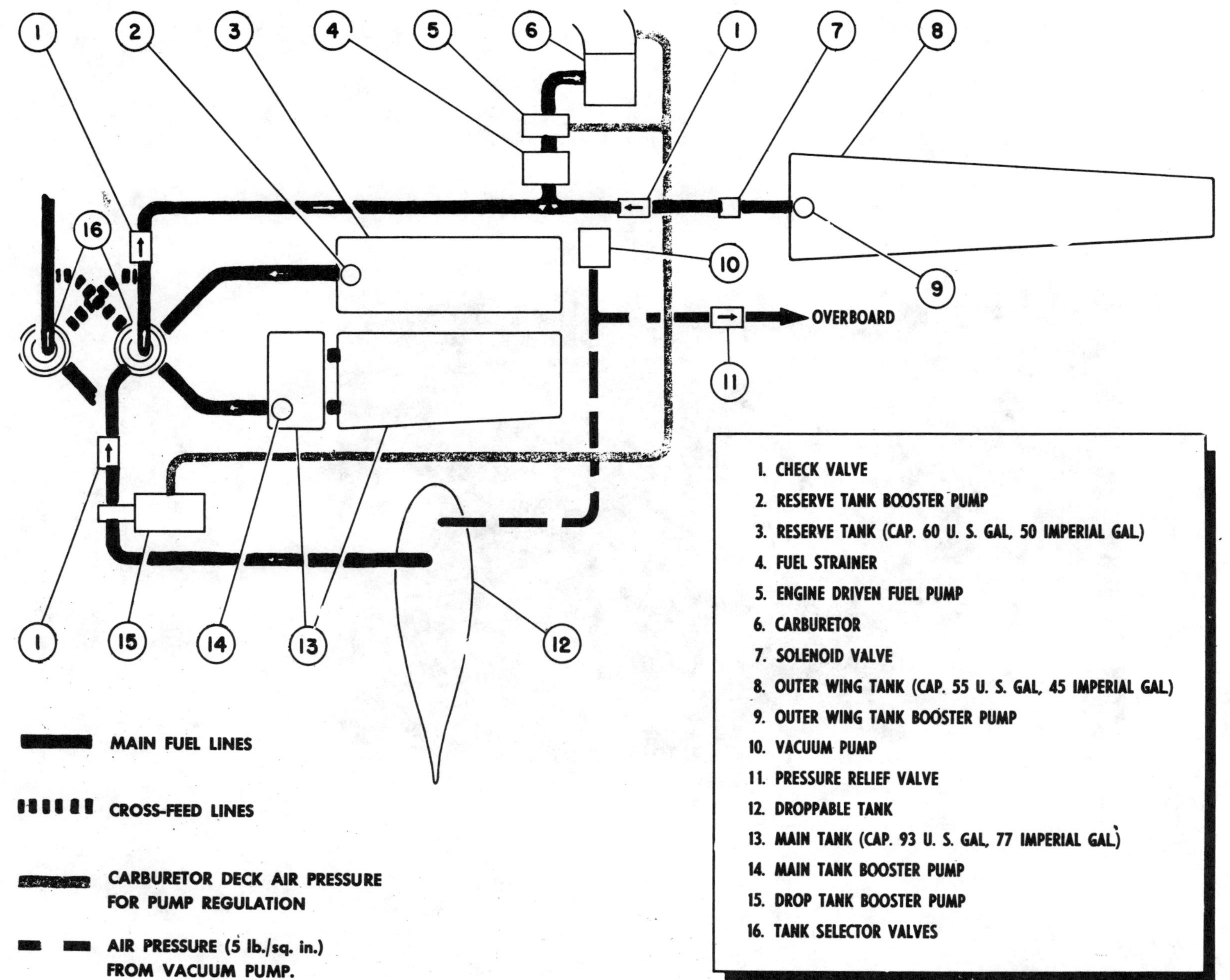

Figure 10A — Simplified Fuel System Diagram (Modified Airplanes)

1. Left-hand tank selector valve.
2. Right-hand tank selector valve.
3. Booster pump speed control switches.
4. Booster pump master switches.

Figure 13A — Fuel System Controls (Modified Airplanes)

1. Electric fuel pump.
2. Surge tank (considered part of main tank).
3. Engine priming pump.
4. Fuel pressure gage.
5. Outlet from tank.
6. Reserve tank (capacity 60 U.S. gal., 50 Imperial gal.).
7. Carburetor.
8. Oil dilution valve.
9. Line to engine primer distributor.
10. Crossfeed valve.
11. Fuel filter.
12. Tank selector valve.
13. Main tank vent.
14. Check valve.
15. Main tank (capacity 93 U.S. gal., 77 Imperial gal.).
16. Passages between main tank and surge tank.
17. Reserve tank vent.
18. Droppable tank (capacity 165 U.S. gal., 137 Imperial gal.).
    Or (300 U.S. gal., 250 Imperial gal).
19. Engine driven fuel pump.
20. Oil dilution line (injects fuel into oil system).
21. Outer wing tank (capacity 55 U.S. gal., 45 Imperial gal.).
    (Not shown in figure 10.)

Key to Figures 10 and 11

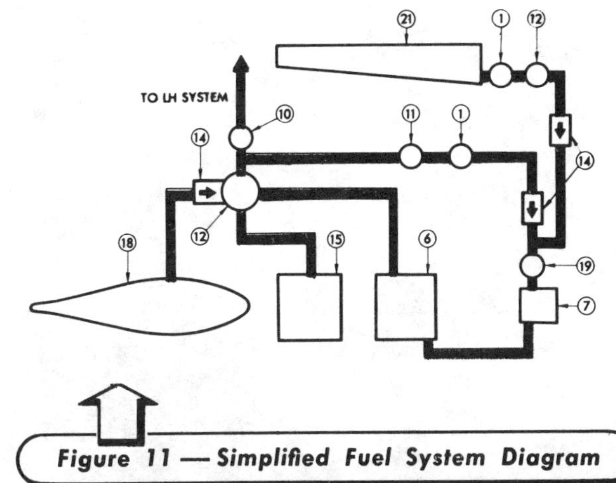

Figure 11 — Simplified Fuel System Diagram

1. Left-hand tank selector valve.
2. Right-hand tank selector valve.
3. Auxiliary fuel pump switches.
4. Outer wing tank low level check button.

Figure 12 — Fuel System Controls (Late Airplanes)

1. Spotlight (in alternate position).
2. Left window crank.
3. Window crank ratchet handle.
4. Electric fuel pump switches.
5. Outer wing tank switches.
6. Crossfeed switch.
7. Shoulder harness release.
8. Right-hand tank selector valve.
9. Left-hand tank selector valve.

Figure 13 — Fuel System Controls (Early Airplanes)

Pump Pressure
Return to Reservoir
Pump Suction
System Pressure
Tank Drain or Vent

1. To coolant flaps (see figure 20). (2)
2. Hydraulic pressure gage.
3. Ground test connections. (2)
4. Check valves. (3)
5. To right-hand engine pump.
6. Flap control valve.
7. Emergency hand pump.
8. To flap system (see figure 16).
9. Main hydraulic reservoir.
10. Engine driven pump.
11. Hydraulic fluid filter.
12. To landing gear (see figure 16).
13. Landing gear control valve.
14. System pressure regulator.
15. Hydraulic pressure accumulator.
16. Vent to atmosphere.
17. Main reservoir drain.

Figure 14 — Basic Hydraulic System Diagram

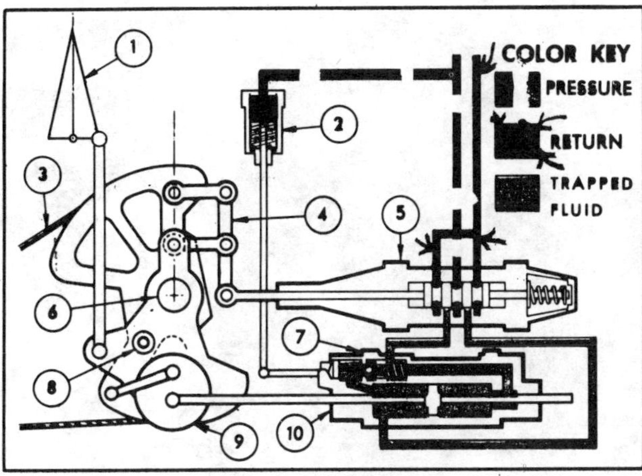

Aileron Neutral

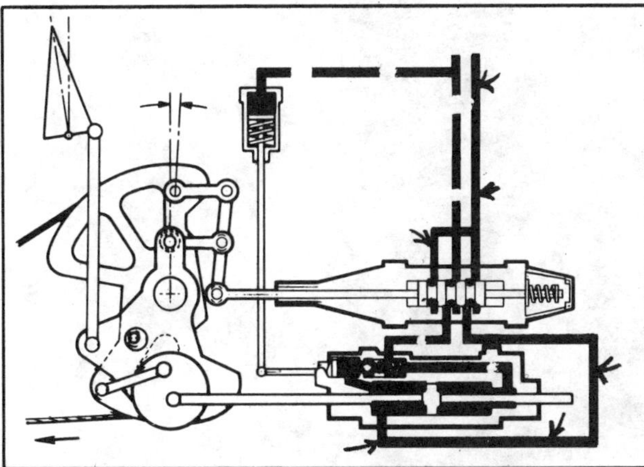

Aileron Moving

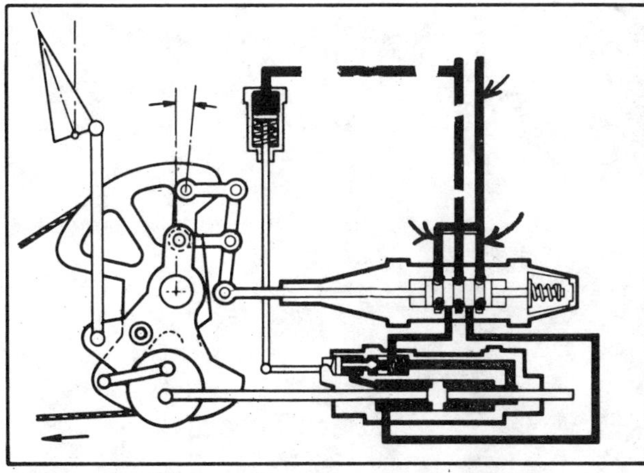

Aileron Movement Completed

1 Aileron.
2. Low pressure by-pass actuator.
3. Control cable.
4. Parallelogram linkage.
5. Control valve.
6. Center pivot point.
7. By-pass valve.
8. Pin in over-size hole.
9. "Feel" lever.
10. Aileron boost cylinder.

Description of Aileron Boost Unit Operation:

In the neutral position, no force is applied to the control cables (figure 15-3) the pin is centered in the oversized hole (figure 15-8) and the control valve (figure 15-5) is closed.

As a force is applied to the control cable, the large control wheel is rotated slightly, the pin is displaced from the center of the oversize hole, and the resultant distortion of the parallelogram linkage (figure 15-4) moves the control valve to one side. This displacement of the control valve allows hydraulic fluid to flow to the boost cylinder (figure 15-10) and assist the original force in moving the aileron.

As the motion of the control wheel is stopped, hydraulic fluid continues to flow to the boost cylinder until the pin is again centered in the hole and the control valve is returned to the OFF position. In this position, the application of force by the pilot continues to act through the feel lever (figure 15-9) and prevents the air loads on the aileron from displacing the pin from the center of the hole.

In the event of failure of the hydraulic pressure, or shutting off the aileron boost shut-off valve (figure 9-5) in the cockpit, the low pressure by-pass actuator cylinder (figure 15-2) moves under spring tension and opens the by-pass valve (figure 15-7). The opening of the by-pass valve allows free flow of fluid from one side of the boost cylinder to the other and prevents the occurrence of a hydraulic lock condition.

With pressure in the boost system thus reduced to zero, full manual operation of the ailerons is obtained when the pin hits the side of the oversize hole (figure 15-8).

Figure 15 — Aileron Boost Unit Diagram

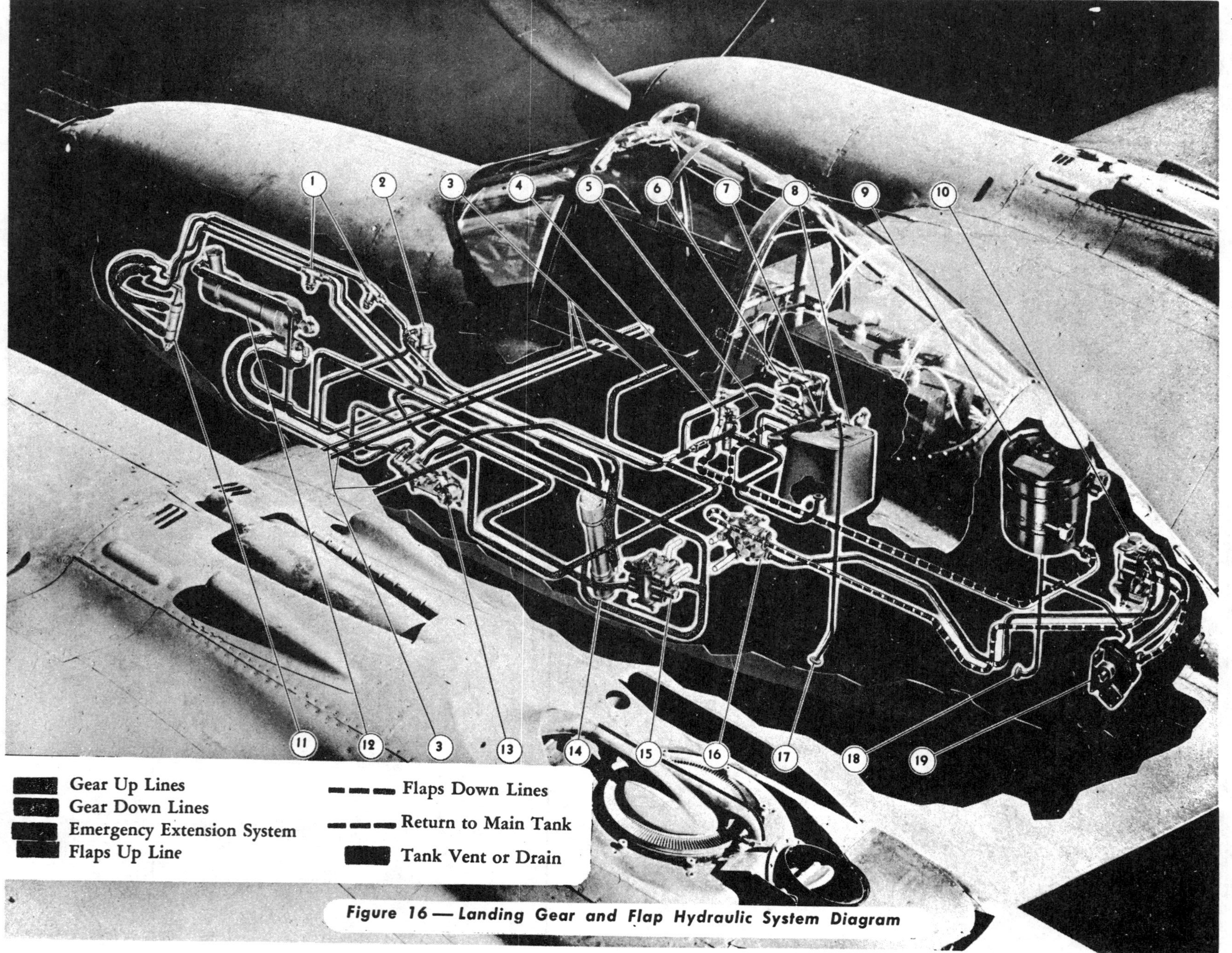

Figure 16 — Landing Gear and Flap Hydraulic System Diagram

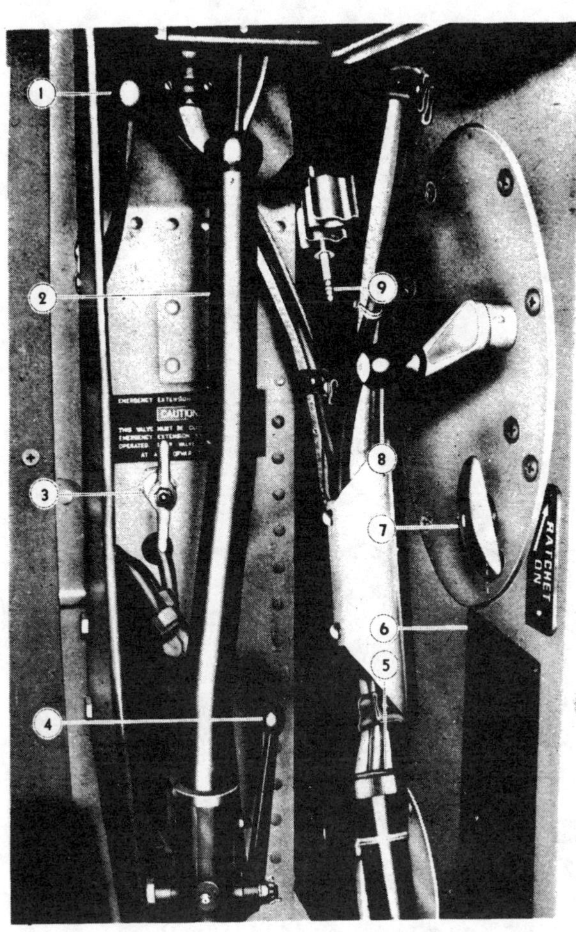

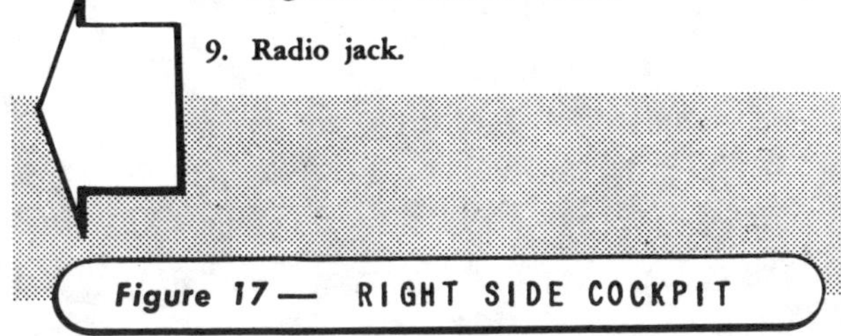

1. Seat adjustment release handle.

2. Hand pump handle.

3. Emergency extension by-pass valve. (Early airplanes only.)

4. Source selector valve handle.

5. Radio jack (stowed position).

6. Emergency extension procedure placard.

7. Window ratchet.

8. Right-hand window crank.

9. Radio jack.

Figure 17 — RIGHT SIDE COCKPIT

1. Combination check and relief valve. (Allows free flow in one direction, high pressure flow in the other direction.)
2. Sequence valve (open only when wheel is UP).
3. Lines to main landing gear system. (2)
4. Emergency extension by-pass valve.
5. Pressure relief valve.
6. Source selector valve (DOWN position).
7. Emergency hand pump.
8. Emergency extension reservoir.
9. Main hydraulic reservoir.
10. Automatic flap stop valve (stops flaps at UP, DOWN, or MANEUVER depending on setting of control lever).
11. Landing gear door locking cylinder.
12. Landing gear extension cylinder (down-lock built in).
13. Landing gear uplock.
14. Landing gear door cylinder.
15. Landing gear control valve.
16. Flap control valve.
17. Vent to atmosphere.
18. Main reservoir drain.
19. Flap motor and gear box.

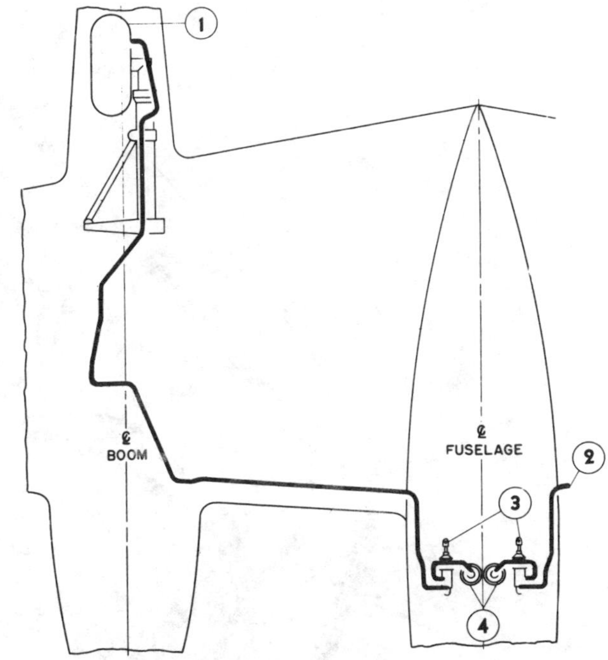

1. Main landing gear wheel and brake.
2. To left-hand gear.
3. Brake cylinders.
4. Hydraulic fluid reservoirs.

Figure 18 — Brake System Diagram

1. Automatic oil temperature regulator.
2. Line to oil pressure gage.
3. Oil tank (capacity 13 U.S. gal., 11 Imperial gal.).
4. Supercharger regulator. (EARLY AIRPLANES ONLY)
5. Vents to atmosphere.
6. Oil from engine.
7. Oil cooling radiators.
8. Oil to engine.

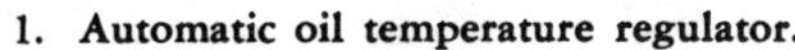

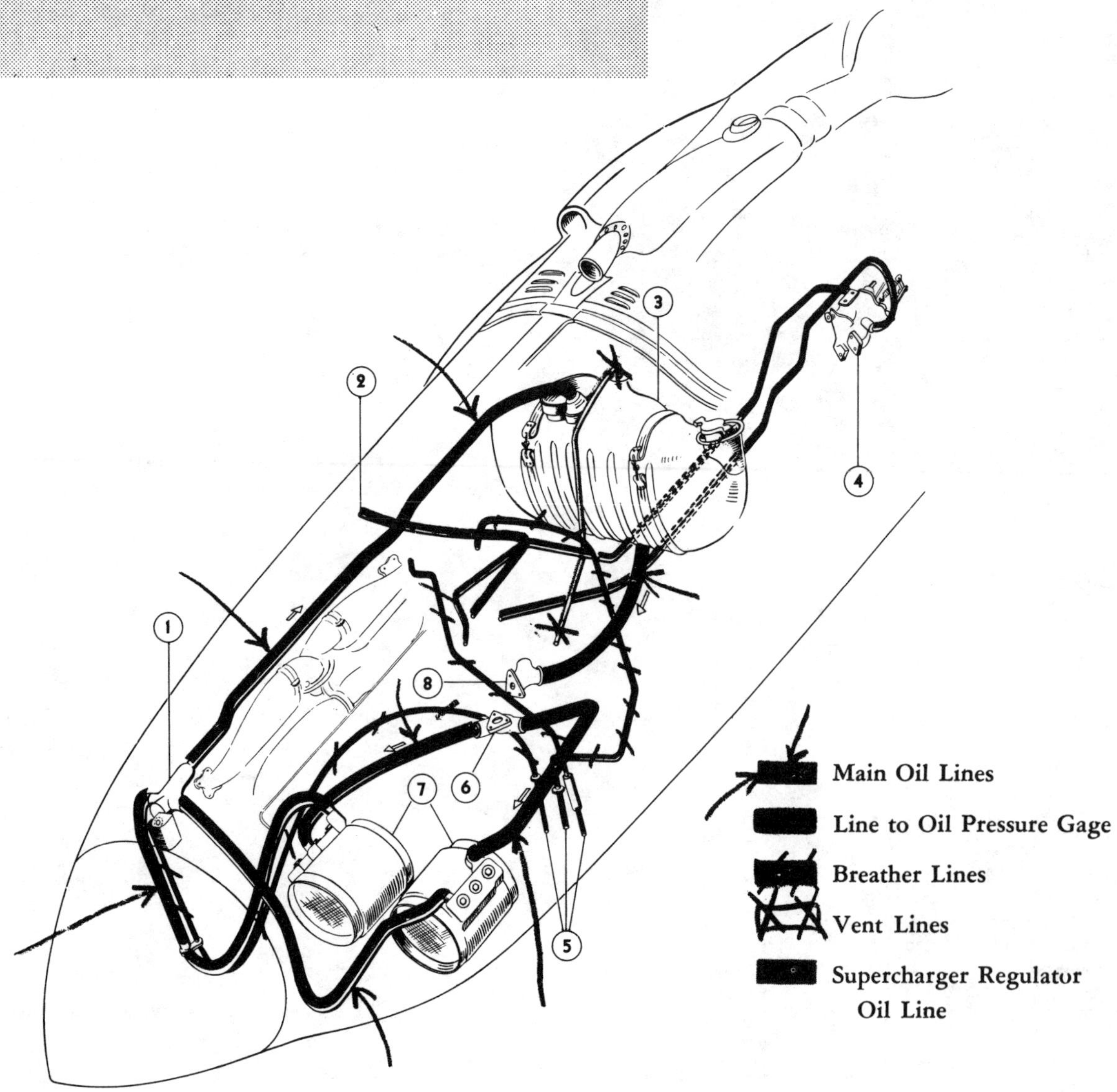

Figure 19 — Oil System Diagram

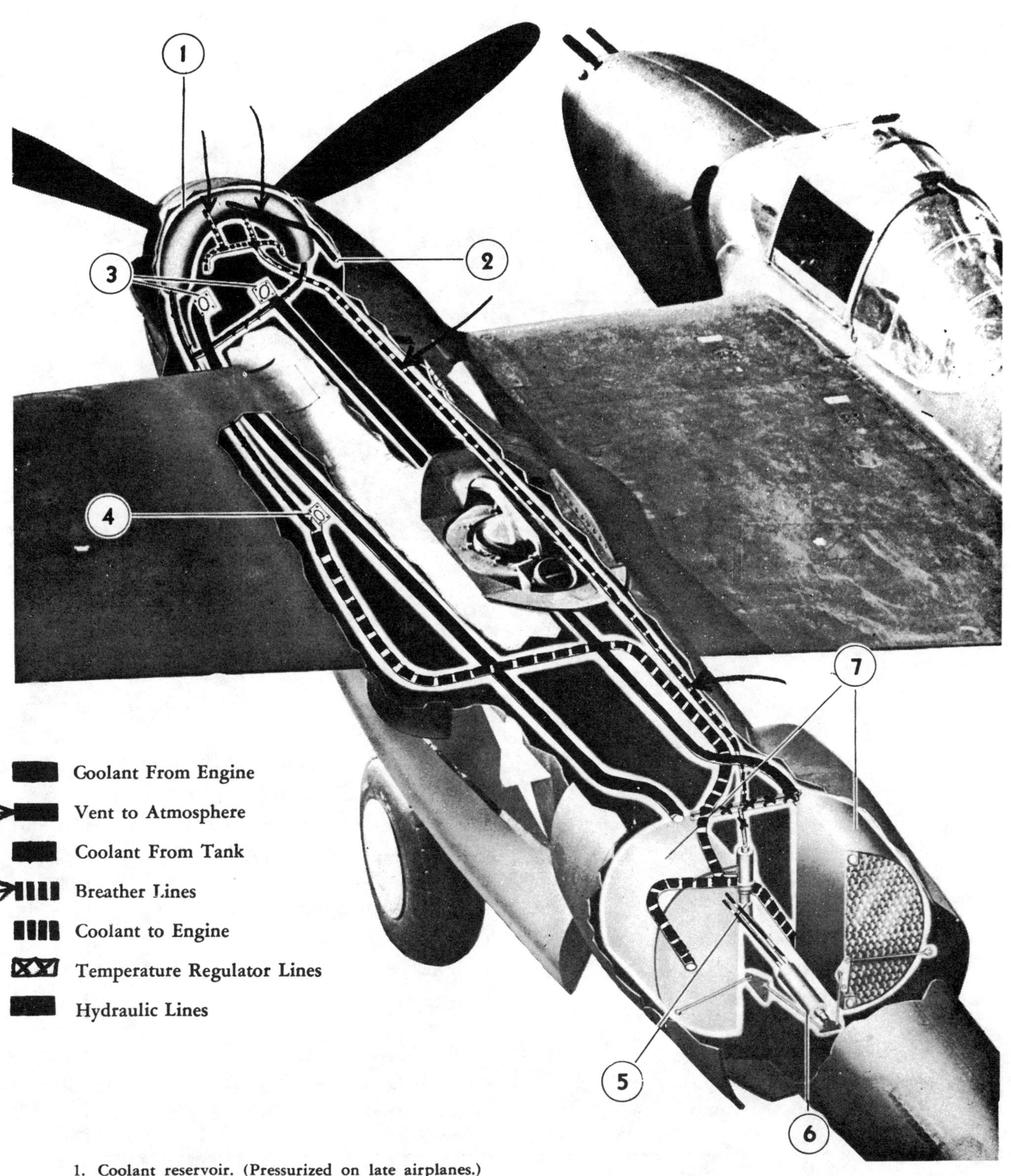

1. Coolant reservoir. (Pressurized on late airplanes.)
2. Vent to atmosphere.
3. Coolant outlet from engine.
4. Coolant inlet to engine.
5. Automatic temperature regulator.
6. Coolant radiator exit flap hydraulic cylinder.
7. Coolant radiators.

Figure 20 — Coolant System Diagram

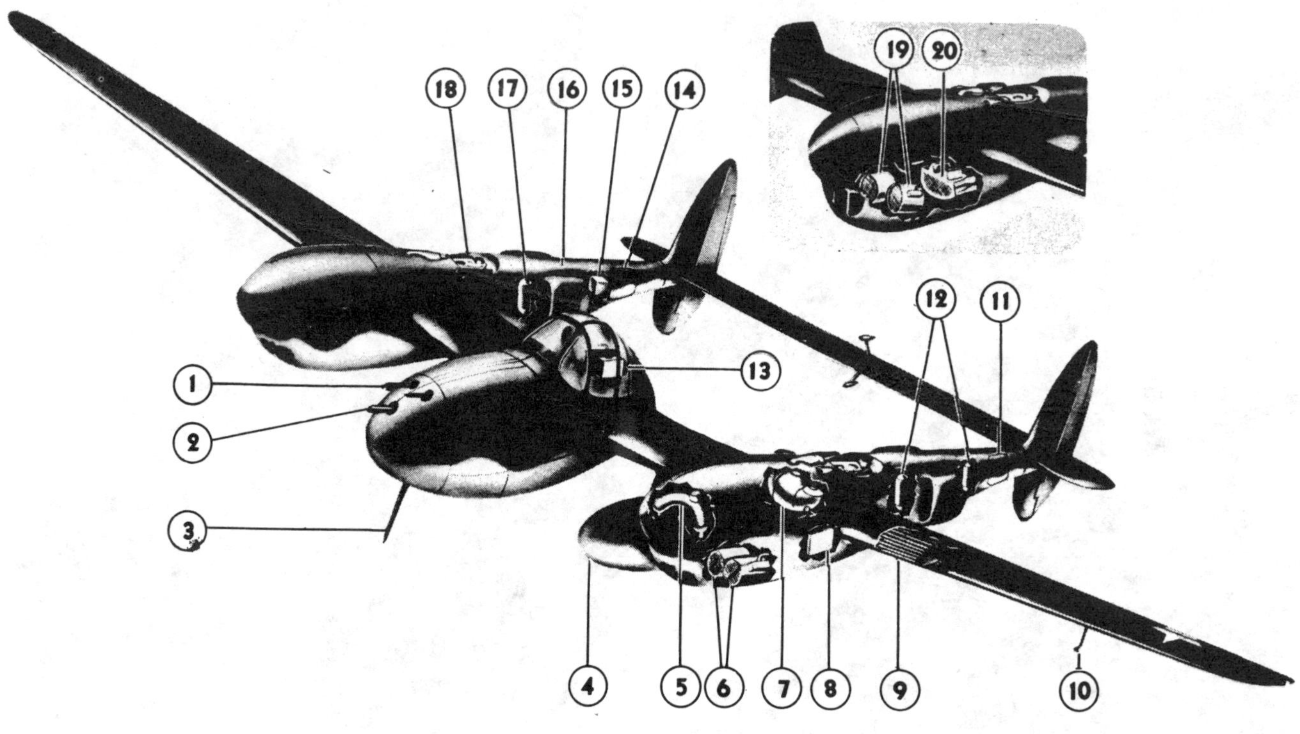

1.	.50 caliber machine guns.	11.	Battery compartment door.
2.	20 mm cannon.	12.	Oxygen bottles.
3.	Antenna mast.	13.	Radio equipment.
4.	Droppable fuel tank.	14.	Baggage compartment door.
5.	Coolant tank.	15.	Recognition radio.
6.	Oil cooler radiators (P-38H).	16.	Coolant radiators.
7.	Oil tank.	17.	Oxygen bottle.
8.	Carburetor air filter.	18.	Turbo supercharger.
9.	Carburetor air intercooler (P-38H).	19.	Oil cooler radiators (P-38J and F-5B).
10.	Airspeed pitot.	20.	Carburetor air intercooler (P-38J and F-5B).

Figure 21 — Airplane Contents Diagram

Pilot Operating Instructions

1. FLIGHT RESTRICTIONS.

a. MANEUVERS PROHIBITED.

(1) Snap rolls and intentional spins.

(2) Continuous inverted flight.

(3) Airspeed or accelerations in excess of those given on the DIVE LIMITS placard (figure 25) which is posted in the cockpit of each airplane. Do not exceed 3.5 G's negative acceleration.

CAUTION

Extreme care must be taken during acrobatic maneuvers which require a downward recovery. Acrobatics should not be attempted at altitudes below 10,000 feet.

b. AIRSPEED LIMITATIONS.

Condition	Maximum Allowable Airspeed (Indicated)
Diving	See Placard (figure 25) Section II paragraph 18
Landing gear extended	175 mph.
Flaps 100% extended	150 mph.
Flaps 50% extended	250 mph.
Landing light extended	140 mph.
300 Gal. droppable tanks installed	250 mph.

2. BEFORE ENTERING PILOT'S COMPARTMENT.

a. Check the loading of the airplane. Determine the approximate take-off weight and the center of gravity position.

WARNING

Dangerous instability exists when the center of gravity is aft of 32% mac. (32% gear up corresponds to 28.5% gear down.) Under these tail heavy conditions, full down elevator will be required to prevent stalling the airplane if the airspeed is allowed to drop below 90 mph indicated with flaps down, power on, and landing gear up.

Note

Tail heavy conditions may be relieved by lowering the landing gear.

b. Check that the cannon and machine guns have been charged and that the radio transmitters have been tuned to the proper frequencies.

c. Access to the airplane is by means of the retractable ladder on the rear of the fuselage (figure 22-5). Push the up-lock release (figure 22-2) and raise the handle (figure 22-4) to a vertical position. Force the handle down until the ladder locks in the position shown. To

1. Flush type handhold.
2. Uplock release.
3. Downlock release.
4. Ladder lever.
5. Ladder.

Figure 22 — Access Ladder

retract the ladder, push the downlock release (figure 22-3) and pull the handle straight up until the ladder stows in place, then swing the handle forward until flush with the fuselage contour, and press firmly into place. A flush, hinged handhold (figure 22-1) is built into the left side of the fuselage.

(1) To open the top hatch, turn the two releases (figure 23-3) on the top of the windshield and rotate the hatch backward.

3. ON ENTERING PILOT'S COMPARTMENT.

a. CHECK FOR ALL FLIGHTS.

(1) Battery switch (figure 5-15) OFF if battery cart is used. ON if cart is not used.

(2) Cross-feed switch (figure 13-6) OFF. (Cross-feed switch is replaced by a cross-feed position of the tank selector valves on later airplanes.)

(3) Turn the tank selector valves to OUTER WING ON (or outer wing tank switches ON).

(a) Check operation of outer wing tank booster pumps by checking the fuel pressure.

(b) Check the condition of the low level warning light bulbs by pushing the test button on the side of the warning light box, or (on modified airplanes) press the bulbs into their sockets.

(4) Oxygen pressure (figure 4-34) 400 to 450 lb/sq in.

(5) Bomb selector switches (figure 4-20) ON and arming switch (figure 4-24) SAFE. (These positions insure that tanks or bombs may be dropped quickly in the event of engine failure at take-off.

(6) Throttles (figure 4-2) 1/10 OPEN. (¾ inch.)

(7) Propeller control (figure 4-4) INC RPM. (Full forward.)

(8) Propeller selector switches (figure 4-5) AUTO CONSTANT SPEED.

(9) Propeller circuit breakers (figure 4-9) ON.

(10) Propeller feathering switches (figure 4-13) NORMAL.

(11) Mixture (figure 4-6) IDLE CUTOFF.

(12) Oil cooler flap switches (figure 5-17) AUTO-MATIC.

(13) Generator switch (figure 5-16 or 8-11) ON.

1. Hatch locking arm (locked position).
2. Hatch release button.
3. External hatch release levers
4. Hatch release handle.
5. Gunsight (late airplanes).
6. Hatch release button.
7. Hatch locking arm (released position).

Figure 23 — Hatch Controls

(14) Coolant flap override switches (figure 5-13) OFF.

(15) Intercooler flaps (figure 5-12) OPEN . (If installed.)

(16) Gun-sight light (figure 5-10) operating and seat adjusted so that the sight reflection is easily visible.

(17) Inverter switch (figure 5-9) (or compass switch on main switch box) ON.

(18) Contactor heater ON if contactor is to be used during the flight.

(19) Armament switch (on control column) OFF.

(20) Fuel quantity (figure 8-20 and 21) adequate. Check the fuel level in outer wing tanks by pressing the low level test button (figure 12-4), or, (on modified airplanes) by operating the low level test switch on the side of the warning light box.

(21) Turbo-supercharger warning lights functioning (if installed).

(22) Carburetor air filters (figure 4-8) AS REQUIRED.

Note

The use of carburetor air filters reduces the critical altitude and range of the airplane and should be avoided in clear air.

(23) Clock and altimeter set.

b. SPECIAL CHECK FOR NIGHT FLYING.—Test by operating.

(1) Landing lights (figure 5-7). (Not more than 5 seconds for test.)

(2) Recognition lights (figure 7-13). (Not more than 10 seconds for test.)

(3) Cockpit lights (figure 5-11).

(4) Fluorescent lights (figure 5-5).

(5) Position lights (figure 5-6).

(6) Spot light (figure 4-1).

4. FUEL SYSTEM MANAGEMENT.

a. GENERAL.—On unmodified airplanes fuel is supplied to each engine by an engine driven fuel pump and one master booster pump which draws fuel from either the main, reserve, or droppable tank depending on the setting of the selector valve. (An additional booster pump for the outer wing tank is installed on airplanes equipped with these tanks.)

On modified airplanes fuel is supplied to each engine by an engine driven fuel pump and an individual booster pump for each tank. The droppable tanks on modified airplanes are also pressurized to 5 lb/sq in.

On all airplanes equipped with outer wing tanks, two low level warning lights are installed on the forward left-hand side of the cockpit. These lights automatically come on when fuel for approximately 5 or 6 minutes of engine operation remains in the tank.

b. NORMAL USE.

(1) Warm up, take off and fly for the first 15 minutes on RESERVE tanks. This is to provide space in the reserve tanks for the vapor return from the carburetors. Switch both engines to the *left* droppable tank until almost dry, then shift to *right* droppable tank until almost dry. Determine hourly fuel consumption from the charts in Appendix II. Fuel gages are not installed in the droppable tanks. Do not drop external tanks unless necessary for increased range or for combat. Use up the fuel in the outer wing tanks (if installed); then use main tanks, and switch back to RESERVE for the remainder of the flight.

WARNING

Always check the fuel level in the tank before trying to operate the engine from that tank. To check the fuel level in the outer wing tanks, press the low level test button (figure 12-4), or, (on modified airplanes), operate the low level test switch on the side of the warning light box. It is not possible to check the fuel level in the droppable tanks.

(2) On unmodified airplanes the booster pumps (figures 12-3, or 13-4) should be operated during take-off and landing to prevent engine failure which may result from engine-driven fuel pump failure. The booster

pumps should also be operated during flight whenever necessary to maintain the required 16 to 18 lb/sq in. fuel pressure.

On modified airplanes the booster pump master switches (figure 13A-4) should be on at all times. The speed control switch should be in the EMERGENCY position during take-off and landing to prevent engine failure which may result from engine-driven fuel pump failure. The booster pumps should also be operated on EMERGENCY whenever necessary during flight to maintain the desired fuel pressure of 16 to 18 lb/sq in. The speed control switches have no effect on the droppable tank booster pumps. On modified airplanes the booster pump switches merely supply power to the booster pumps. The proper pump is turned on by contacts on the tank selector valve.

Note

Never exceed 250 mph indicated with 300 gallon droppable tanks installed.

(3) To release droppable fuel tanks:

(a) Raise flaps and landing gear.

(b) Turn tank selector valves (figures 13-8 and 13-9) to MAIN, RESERVE, or OUTER WING.

(c) Move arming switch (figure 4-24) to ARM or SAFE.

(d) Turn selector switches (figure 4-20) ON for tank(s) to be dropped.

(e) Press the release button (figure 4-27) when flying at an angle not greater than 30° from the horizontal.

Note

An emergency droppable tank or bomb release control is installed in late airplanes. It is located either behind and to the left of the seat or directly in front of the pilot's seat.

(f) Full fuel tanks may be dropped without danger at airspeeds up to 400 mph. Empty 150 gallon tanks should be dropped only while flying at an airspeed of 160 mph or less. On late airplanes, droppable tanks are equipped with displacement struts which increase the safe dropping speed to 350 mph.

WARNING

EMPTY 300 GALLON TANKS ARE TO BE DROPPED ONLY IN AN EMERGENCY as the tanks may hit the airplane when released. To drop the tanks, it is necessary to slow the airplane down to 120 mph with landing gear and flaps up to avoid serious damage.

b. LONG RANGE FERRY FLIGHT.

(1) Whenever flying with droppable tanks, it is advisable to operate both engines from the LEFT droppable tank until empty and then operate both engines from the RIGHT droppable tank. This procedure empties the left tank in the minimum time and, if necessary, it can be released sooner than by operating each engine from its own individual tank.

c. CROSS FEED OPERATION.

(1) On early airplanes the left and right fuel systems are connected by an electrically operated "crossfeed" valve which makes it possible to operate either engine from any tank, except the outer wing tank. Late airplanes have a crossfeed position on the tank selector valves. When prolonged single engine flight makes it necessary to use fuel from the dead engine side, or when operating both engines from one droppable tank, operate the fuel system as follows:

(a) Airplanes with four-way fuel tank selector valves.

1. Turn tank selector valve to the tank to supply fuel.

2. Turn crossfeed switch (figure 13-6) to CROSSFEED.

3. Turn other tank selector valve OFF.

(b) Airplanes with five-way fuel tank selector valves.

1. Turn tank selector valve to the tank to supply fuel.

2. Turn other tank selector valve to CROSS-SUCTION.

Note

It is not possible to cross-feed fuel from the outer wing tanks.

CAUTION

Do not attempt to use the booster pumps on modified airplanes during cross-feed operation if there is a leak in the fuel lines to the dead engine. The booster pumps will pressurize the fuel lines, forcing fuel out through the leak.

5. STARTING ENGINES.

Note

Engine fire extinguishers are NOT installed in this airplane. Strict adherence to the following instructions as to mixture control positions will reduce the possibility of fire. If fire does occur, shut off mixture control, tank selector valve, electric fuel pump, and ignition to the affected engine.

a. With ignition OFF and mixture controls at IDLE CUT OFF, turn the engines over by hand two or three revolutions if they have been idle for more than three hours.

b. On unmodified airplanes check the operation of the fuel booster pumps (figure 12-3 or 13-4). The fuel pressure with the engines not operating should be 15 to 16 lb/sq in. On modified airplanes check the operation of the fuel booster pumps (figure 14A-3 and 4) on each tank. The fuel pressures with the engines not operating should be as follows:

(1) With the speed control switches on NORMAL —8 to 10 lb/sq in. on any tank except the droppable tanks.

(2) With the speed control switches on EMERGENCY—16 to 18 lb/sq in. on any tank except the droppable tanks.

(3) Droppable tank fuel pressure — 15 to 16 lb/sq in.

c. Turn the booster pumps on unmodified airplanes OFF after above test. On modified airplanes, leave booster pumps ON and return the speed control switches to NORMAL.

d. Return the tank selector valves to RES. ON and prime the left engine. On unmodified airplanes, push the primer handle down, turn 90° to unlock, and prime two to four strokes. On modified airplanes, hold the priming-oil dilution switch (figure 5-2) in the aft position two to four seconds.

Note

Priming time will be shortened if the booster pumps are on EMERGENCY.

e. Turn ignition master switch (figure 5-1) ON.

f. Turn left ignition switch (figure 5-18) to BOTH.

g. Hold the starter switch (figure 5-3) to LH (left-hand) until the inertia starter has reached maximum rpm.

h. Push the engage switch (figure 5-4) to LH, still holding starter switch to LH, and prime as required.

i. As soon as the engine definitely fires, place the mixture control (figure 4-6) to AUTO RICH.

Note

It may be necessary to operate the electric fuel pumps for a short while if the engine driven pumps do not build up pressure immediately.

j. Return the mixture control to IDLE CUTOFF if the engine does not continue to run.

k. Stop the engine if oil pressure does not register within 30 seconds.

l. Start the right-hand engine by repeating the preceding paragraphs 5f through j.

m. Lock the primer pump DOWN.

n. Turn battery switch (figure 5-15) ON before disconnecting the battery cart.

Note

If battery power is not sufficient for starting, use the inertia starter handcrank or an external energizer. The handcrank is stowed in left main landing gear wheel-well.

6. ENGINE WARM-UP AND ACCESSORY CHECK.

a. Keep the RPM under 1400 until the oil temperature reaches 40°C (105°F) or shows a definite increase of 10°C (18°F) and the oil pressure is steady below 75 lb/sq in.

b. While the engines are warming up, test the communication equipment with the control tower, or with another airplane.

7. EMERGENCY TAKE-OFF.

a. When necessary, take-off may be made without the normal engine and accessories ground tests *provided* that the oil pressure is steady below 85 lb/sq in. and that the oil temperature has shown a definite increase of at least 10°C (18°F) since starting. If necessary, use the oil dilution system to reduce the oil pressure.

b. Over-dilution is likely to result from diluting the oil in a cold engine. If dilution is necessary during warm-up, oil pressure should be carefully watched during the remainder of warm-up and during take-off to insure that over-dilution has not occurred.

8. ENGINE AND ACCESSORIES OPERATION GROUND TEST.

a. Extend and retract the flaps (figure 7-2) to check

the operation of the hydraulic system. When both engines are operating at 1400 RPM, fifteen to twenty seconds is the normal extension time; twenty-five seconds is the normal extension time if only one engine is operating at 1400 RPM.

b. Check for normal fuel pressure (figures 8-7 and 8-14) 16 to 18 lb/sq in. with electric fuel pumps OFF. Check for idling pressure of 9 lb/sq in.

c. Increase RPM to 2300.

(1) Check propeller control levers (figure 4-4) DEC RPM then INC RPM (full forward).

(2) Check propeller selector switches (figure 4-5) DEC RPM then INC RPM, then return to AUTO CONSTANT SPEED. Be sure that propeller warning lights (on P-38H only) glow when selector switches are out of AUTO CONSTANT SPEED.

(3) Check magnetos. Maximum normal drop, 100 RPM after shifting from both to either left or right magneto. *Engine must run smoothly on either magneto.*

(4) With the generator switch (two on later airplanes) ON, check the voltmeter (figure 5-8) for approximately 28 volts and the ammeter (two on later airplanes) (figure 8-12) for charge.

(5) Move intercooler flap controls to OPEN (if installed) and check operation of turbo-superchargers by opening throttles individually to take-off power (see specific engine Flight Chart in Section III).

CAUTION

Do not operate engines at take-off power for more than two or three seconds while on the ground.

d. Type A-4 Automatic Pilot (F-5B only).

(1) Check vacuum (figure 8-2) 4″ to 5″ Hg.

(2) Check automatic-pilot oil pressure (figure 33-10) 125 lb/sq in.

(3) Check the artificial horizon unit uncaged (figure 24-5).

(4) Match the directional gyro cards on the directional gyro (figure 24-6).

(5) Turn the automatic-pilot control valve (figure 24-10) ON.

(6) Turn the course setting knob (figure 24-4), the elevator trim knob (figure 24-9), and the aileron trim knob (figure 24-7) to check operation of the units.

(7) TURN AUTOMATIC PILOT CONTROL VALVE *OFF* BEFORE TAKE-OFF.

9. TAXIING INSTRUCTIONS.

The airplane taxis easily and forward visibility is good. Use differential throttle control for turning to save the brakes. There is no danger of nose over or ground loop should it become necessary to turn sharply or to apply full brakes.

WATCH WHERE YOU'RE GOING WHEN TAXIING*!!*

10. TAKE-OFF.

a. Check the following:

(1) Top hatch—LOCKED IN PLACE. Side windows—cranked (figure 13-2) CLOSED. Side window ratchets (figure 13-3)—ON.

Note

Open side windows will cause buffeting of the tail section.

(2) Propeller levers (figure 4-4) INC RPM (full forward).

(3) Propeller selector switches (figure 4-5) AUTO CONSTANT SPEED.

(4) Mixture (figure 4-6)—AUTO RICH.

(5) Tank selector valves (figures 13-8 and 13-9) RESERVE ON.

(6) Dive flaps (figure 9-2)—UP. (P-38L and late P-38J airplanes.)

(7) Wing flaps UP. Wing flap lever (figure 7-2) CLOSED. Up to ½ flaps may be used for short take-off run.)

(8) Flight controls free and proper movement.

Note

Look at surfaces for this check-to see that they move in the right direction.

(9) Aileron boost shut-off valve (figure 9-5) ON. Aileron boost should be on at all times. Turn off only in case of emergency.

WARNING

Never turn the aileron boost shut-off valve from OFF to ON during flight.

Note

A slight "nibbling" at the control wheel may be noticed on take-off. This is because retraction of the landing gear may reduce the hydraulic system pressure below 200 lb/sq in. If the system pressure falls below this value, the aileron boost will become inoperative. As the pump increases the pressure, the "nibbling" may be noticed when the boost again becomes effective.

(10) Generator switch(es) (figure 5-16 or 8-11) ON.

(11) Intercooler flaps (figure 5-12) OPEN if installed).

(12) Droppable tanks or bombs prepared for immediate dropping by turning bomb selector switches (figure 4-20) ON and arming switch (figure 4-24) to SAFE.

(13) Fuel booster pumps (figures 12-3, 13-4, or 13A-3) ON. Booster pump speed control switches (figure 13A-4) EMERGENCY. (Speed control switches are on modified airplanes only.)

(14) Rudder, elevator tab 3° back and aileron tabs ZERO.

(15) Taxi a few feet *straight* down the runway so that the nose wheel will be in line when take-off power is applied. Maximum performance take-offs require holding the airplane with brakes at the end of the runway until engine power reaches the desired setting. Because of the tricycle landing gear, there is no tendency for the airplane to take-off by itself, and no feeling of lightness as take-off speed is reached. Start to ease the control column back at about 70 mph, then at 90 or 100 lift the airplane into the air.

(16) Hold brakes, open throttles to 46″ Hg. 3000 RPM.

(17) Release brakes and keep manifold pressure below 54″ Hg.

CAUTION

Be prepared to reduce power immediately to prevent uncontrollable yaw and roll in case of failure of one engine during take-off.

(18) Retract landing gear as soon as practical after leaving the ground.

Note

Retract the landing gear immediately after the airplane is off the ground so that the flight may be safely continued in the event of one-engine failure after take-off.

(19) Reduce manifold pressure to 43″ Hg. at 2600 rpm after clearing all obstacles.

11. ENGINE FAILURE DURING TAKE-OFF.

a. If one engine fails before the airplane leaves the ground, close both throttles immediately and apply full brakes. If it is going to be impossible to stop on the runway, retract the landing gear by turning the landing gear control release knob and raising the landing gear lever.

b. If one engine fails after the airplane leaves the ground, but before the safe single-engine airspeed (120 mph) has been reached, close both throttles and LAND STRAIGHT AHEAD. Retract the landing gear if it is not possible to land on the runway.

c. If one engine fails after reaching the safe airspeed of 120 mph and after the landing gear has started up:

(1) Reduce power enough to regain control, then apply power gradually. Hold enough rudder to prevent the airplane from skidding and hold the wings level.

(2) Release droppable tanks or bombs over an unpopulated area.

(3) Trim rudder tabs.

(4) Set the mixture on the dead engine to IDLE CUT-OFF.

Note

Do not apply so much power that the airplane cannot be held straight with the rudder. A manifold pressure of 45″ Hg. at 3000 RPM should be enough to accelerate the airplane to a good single engine climbing airspeed of 165 mph.

(5) Feather the dead engine's propeller.

(6) Turn OFF electric fuel pump of dead engine.

(7) Circle the field and land, do not make turns into the dead engine unless trim and speed have been establish.

12. CLIMB.

a. Mixture (figure 4-6) AUTO RICH.

b. Intercooler flaps (figure 5-12) OPEN (if installed).

c. Refer to the Take-off, Climb and Landing Chart in Appendix II for the best climbing speeds at different weights, powers and altitudes. The average best-climbing-speed at sea level is 160 mph.

d. On P-38H airplanes, carburetor air temperature is critical in a high power climb between 15,000 and 25,000 feet. Above 25,000 feet turbo-supercharger overspeed is critical. Excessive temperatures will cause detonation and very rough engine operation resulting in loss of power and probable engine damage.

(1) On P-38J, P-38L, and F-5B airplanes *with intercooler flaps OPEN,* the manifold pressure is limited by the rating of the engine up to 25,000 feet. Above 25,000 feet, turbo-supercharger overspeed is again critical.

e. The following maximum manifold pressures are to be used for "War Emergency" only. *Never exceed 60 inches Hg.* In a climb above 25,000 feet these limits indicate the approximate values at which the turbo-supercharger warning lights should glow. In level flight it should be possible to obtain the manifold pressure shown below at slightly higher altitudes.

Altitude Feet	P-38H		P-38J, P-38L and F-5B
	B-13 turbo	B-33 turbo	B-33 turbo
up to 7,000	60	60	60
20,000	55	55	60
25,000	45	52	60
30,000	35	49	53
35,000	30	44	45
40,000	20	36	37

Early P-38H airplanes are equipped with type B-13 turbo-superchargers. Later P-38H airplanes and P-38J, P-38L, and F-5B airplanes are equipped with type B-33 turbo-superchargers.

f. Refer to the Specific Engine Flight Chart in Section III for power time limitations.

g. Refer to the Take-off, Climb and Landing Chart in Appendix II for rate of climb. Note correction to be made during hot weather.

13. GENERAL FLYING CHARACTERISTICS.

a. Due to the counter-rotating propellers, there is no noticeable torque effect in any two engine flying with this airplane. Rudder and aileron trim tab settings do not require adjustment as a result of changes in airspeed and power.

b. TO INCREASE POWER IN FLIGHT.

(1) Move mixture controls (figure 4-6) to AUTO RICH if maximum cruising power is to be exceeded (see Specific Engine Flight Chart in Section III).

(2) Move propeller controls (figure 4-4) to the new RPM.

(3) Move throttles (figure 4-2) to the new manifold pressure.

c. TO DECREASE POWER IN FLIGHT.

(1) Move throttles (figure 4-2) to the new manifold pressure.

(2) Move propeller controls (figure 4-4) to the new RPM.

(3) Re-adjust the throttles.

(4) Move mixture controls (figure 4-6) to AUTO LEAN if permissible.

d. The turbo-superchargers are controlled by the same levers which operate the throttles. On P-38H, F-5B, and early P-38J airplanes supercharger overspeed is indicated by warning lights. Rated turbo-supercharger speed is 24,000 RPM and overspeed is 26,400 RPM allowable for 5 minutes. The warning lights start to flicker at 25,600 turbo-supercharger RPM and burn continuously at 26,400 RPM. Operation within the flickering range is permissible only during "War Emergencies" and the throttles must be retarded when the flicker changes to continuous burning. P-38L and late P-38J airplanes are equipped with supercharger regulators incorporating an overspeed control and on these airplanes overspeed warning lights are not installed.

e. On P-38J, P-38L, and F-5B airplanes the intercooler flaps should be open for take-off and climbs and nearly closed at all other times. Carburetor air temperature should not be allowed to exceed 45°C (113°F). P-38H airplanes are not equipped with intercooler flaps.

f. Flight operations should be planned from the Flight Operations Instructions Charts in Appendix II. When using these charts, make sure that the chart being used is applicable to the airplane. Charts are clearly marked to indicate the airplane model, the weight, and the external load items carried. If the weight or external load is to be changed during the flight, be sure to use the proper charts.

g. The airplane is stable at all normal speeds. The airplane becomes slightly nose-heavy when the flaps and landing gear are extended. Release of droppable fuel tanks causes no noticeable change. Two-engine cruising below 170 mph indicated airspeed is not recommended because the airplane requires more attention and range is not increased.

14. AUTOMATIC PILOT OPERATING INSTRUCTIONS. (F-5B Only)

a. Trim the airplane for "hands off" flight.

b. Set the directional gyro (lower) card to agree with the compass and rotate the course setting knob until the upper and lower cards coincide.

c. Check the directional gyro. (Uncaged)

d. Turn the automatic pilot elevator and aileron trim knobs to zero.

e. Turn the automatic pilot control valve ON.

f. Adjust the course setting knob and the trim knobs to hold the airplane in straight and level flight.

g. Adjust the speed valves (figure 24-2) to obtain the proper rate of control.

h. Disengage automatic pilot every 15 minutes in flight to reset the directional gyro with the compass and retrim the airplane for "hands off" flight.

i. Make small directional changes (flat turns) by turning the course setting knobs slowly to the new heading.

j. Make faster turns by setting the airplane in a bank with aileron trim knob, caging the directional gyro, and rotating the course setting knob until the ball bank indicator is centered.

CAUTION

The operating limits are 55° in a climb or dive and 90° in a bank. Both gyros should be caged during any maneuvers which might exceed these limits.

15. STALLS.

a. With power OFF, the airplane stalls at the following indicated airspeeds at the gross weight noted:

	15,000 lb.	*17,000 lb.*	*19,000 lb.*
Flaps and landing gear UP	94 mph	100 mph	105 mph
Flaps and landing gear DOWN	69 mph	74 mph	78 mph

b. As stalling speed is approached, the center section stalls first with noticeable shaking of the airplane, however, the ailerons remain effective.

c. In either "power-on" or "power-off" stalls with flaps and landing gear up, the airplane "mushes" straight forward in a well-controlled stall. With flaps and landing gear down, there appears to be a slight tendency for one wing to drop. There is, however, no tendency to spin. Under these conditions, the nose drops slightly and, as the speed increases, the wing will come up.

16. SPINS.

a. Deliberate spinning is prohibited because the spin tends to flatten out after two or three turns. When this occurs, the control column is forced back and engine power must be used to help get the control column forward. Before flattening out, normal recovery may be made without power. Recovery is made by applying full opposite rudder and easing the control column forward.

17. ACROBATICS.

CAUTION

Cage all gyro instruments before engaging in acrobatics.

a. Although such maneuvers as loops, Immelmanns, and rolls are permitted with this airplane, the pilot is cautioned to exercise extreme care in acrobatic maneuvers which require a downward recovery as the loss of altitude in downward recovery is very rapid. In general, acrobatics should *not* be attempted at altitudes below 10,000 feet until the pilot becomes familiar with the speed at which the airplane can gain and lose altitude.

18. DIVING.

CAUTION

Manifold pressure must be kept at or above 20 inches Hg. during extended shallow dives in order to prevent possible malfunctioning or misfiring of engines when throttles are opened after the pullout from the dive. In steep dives with dive recovery flaps extended the throttles may be closed completely without danger.

<table>
<tr><td>

1. Rate control (ground adjustment only).
2. Speed valves—(3).
3. Course setting knob indicator.
4. Course setting knob.
5. Artificial horizon caging knob.

</td><td>

6. Directional gyro caging knob.
7. Aileron trim knob.
8. Miniature airplane control.
9. Elevator trim knob.
10. Automatic pilot control valve.

</td></tr>
</table>

Figure 24 — Automatic Pilot Controls

a. The diving speed is restricted as indicated on the placard (figure 25)—a copy of which is posted in the cockpit of each airplane. As the airplane approaches the critical speed, it becomes rapidly nose heavy and starts to buffet as if it were about to stall. If this condition is allowed to develop, the nose heavy condition will become more pronounced, and it will be very difficult to pull out.

b. The speed at which the above condition occurs depends upon the altitude and the acceleration (or G's)

which is being applied in a pullout. Figure 25 shows the placard consisting of three curves of indicated airspeed plotted against acceleration and indicates the safe range at the altitudes shown on each curve.

c. For example: If a straight dive is made in excess of 360 mph (indicated) at 20,000 feet, the airplane will become nose heavy and start to buffet. Or if a pullout of over 4.5 G's is made at 300 mph at 20,000 feet, the same condition will be evident.

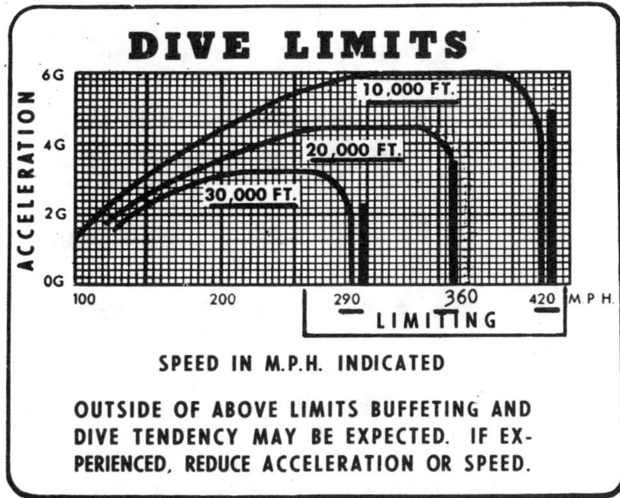

Figure 25 — Dive Placard

d. When the above conditions are noticed, the following action should be taken immediately.

(1) In accelerated maneuvers (dive pullouts or steep turns) buffeting may be stopped by reducing the acceleration.

(2) In steady dives at high speed, buffeting may be stopped by reducing the airplane speed and pulling out using minimum acceleration. Use the elevator tab (figure 4-35) if necessary to assist recovery.

WARNING

Elevator tab must be used with care in order to prevent an extreme tail heavy condition after buffeting stops.

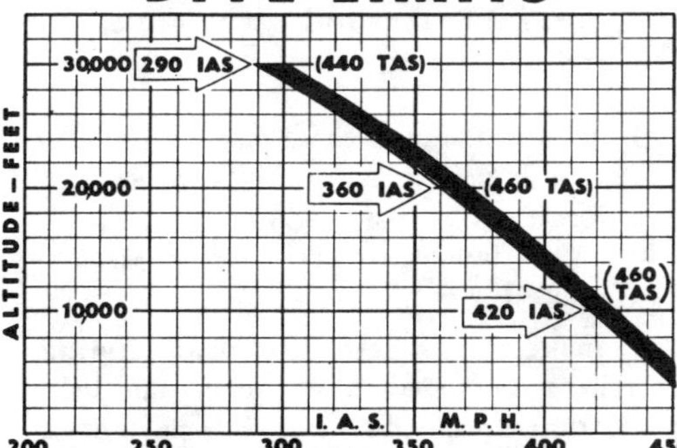

Figure 25A — Dive Placard

e. A new placard (figure 25A) will be installed in late airplanes and may be made retroactive to airplanes already in service. This new placard indicates the safe speed range at any altitude for one G flight. As the airplane approaches this critical one G condition, its ability to pull out is gradually reduced and at the critical speed, buffeting and nose heaviness will occur.

f. DIVE RECOVERY FLAPS.—P-38L and Later P38J airplanes are provided with dive recovery flaps to improve the dive recovery characteristics of the airplane. As described above, the airplane without these flaps becomes very nose heavy and starts to buffet above placard dive speeds. This condition is caused by a high speed stall and a consequent decrease in lift in the wing producing the nose heavy condition. The dive recovery flaps which are installed under the wings between the booms and the ailerons, restore the lift to this portion of the wing and thus cause the uncontrollable nose heaviness to occur at a higher speed. The flaps also add some drag to the airplane, which in conjunction with the higher allowable dive speed, permits safe dives at a much steeper diving angle. The dive recovery flaps should be extended before starting the dive or immediately after the dive has started before a buffeting speed has been reached. If the airplane is buffeting before the dive recovery flaps are extended, the buffeting will momentarily increase and then diminish. With these flaps extended, the nose heaviness is definitely reduced but the diving speed should never be allowed to exceed the placard by more than 15 or 20 mph. With the dive recovery flaps extended before entering the dive, angles of dive up to 45° may be safely accomplished. Without dive recovery flaps extended, the maximum angle for extended dives is 15°. Diving characteristics are better with power off than with power on.

WARNING

Although the dive recovery flaps greatly improve the diving characteristics of the airplane, dangerous buffeting and nose heaviness will still be encountered at diving angles above 45° if the diving speed is allowed to exceed the placard limits by more than 15 to 20 mph.

19. NIGHT FLYING.

a. Very little light need be used for normal cruising flight as all instrument dials are coated with phosphorescent paint. Fluorescent lights (figure 5-5) should be dimmed down until the instruments are barely visible. This will enable the eyes to become accustomed to the darkness. The instrument glare shield should be installed for all night flying.

b. When more light is needed, cockpit lights (figure 5-11) may be turned on, or the spotlight (figure 4-1) may be focused on any point where local light is desired and adjusted to the required brilliancy.

c. Position lights are turned on by a switch (figure 5-6) on the main switch box.

d. Landing lights (figure 5-7) may be used for take-off and landing. They should not, however, be extended at any time when the airspeed is greater than 140 mph.

e. Recognition lights may be used as required.

20. APPROACH AND LANDING.

a. GENERAL.—The landing technique is similar to that of airplanes with conventional tricycle landing gear and the landing attitude is about the same; i.e., main wheels first, tail slightly down.

Note

Extreme tail-low landings, possible only with flaps UP, may cause the fins to strike the runway.

(1) With the landing gear DOWN and flaps at MANEUVER, start the approach at 120 mph indicated air speed. When the approach is assured, put the flaps all the way down, come over the fence at 110 mph, flare off to about 80 mph and wait for contact.

(2) If, for some reason, the flaps cannot be lowered, land a little faster and allow for more flare-off and a flatter gliding angle.

b. NORMAL LANDING.

(1) Tank selector valves (figures 13-8 and 13-9) to MAIN or RESERVE, whichever contains the most fuel.

(2) Mixture controls (figure 4-6) AUTO RICH.

(3) Propeller levers (figure 4-4) to about 2600 rpm position.

(4) Electric fuel pumps (figure 13-4) ON.

(5) Landing gear (figure 4-32) DOWN (not over 175 mph).

(6) Pump the brake pedals a few times to insure that brakes are working.

(7) Wing flaps (figure 7-2) DOWN (not over 150 mph).

Note

Lift the flap lever trigger through the quadrant notch to place lever to DOWN.

(8) Intercooler flaps (figure 5-12) OPEN unless operating in extreme low temperatures. (If installed.)

(9) Flaps UP before taxiing.

c. CROSS WIND LANDING.

(1) Same as the normal landing. The tricycle landing gear reduces danger of groundlooping from landing in a reasonably strong cross wind. If the drift seems excessive, the up-wind wing may be lowered until just before contact.

d. SINGLE ENGINE APPROACH AND LANDING.

CAUTION

Concentrate sharply on your approach—because once you have fully extended the flaps, and the landing gear or descended below five hundred feet, you cannot again circle the field and you must make a landing. If, however, the flaps are not fully extended and your elevation is still five hundred feet or more, and you want to go around again, proceed as follows before beginning to circle:

Apply as much power as can be held, at the same time retracting the landing gear, Accelerate to at least 160 mph, and Raise the flaps (unless they are already fully raised).

Do not make turns into the dead engine unless trim and speed have been establish. It is recommended that the inexperienced pilot practice single engine landing by completely closing one throttle and setting the corresponding propeller lever to the "DE-CREASE RPM" (full rear) position. With this procedure the throttle engine will present nearly the same drag as a feathered propeller and if necessary both throttles may be opened to go around. Don't forget to push the propeller levers forward if it is necessary to go around.

(1) Secure radio clearance for emergency landing.

(2) Turn aileron control booster OFF to conserve hydraulic power for landing gear and flap operation.

(3) Start approach allowing 1000 feet above field for each two miles away.

(4) Extend landing gear at 160 mph.

Note

Allow more time for landing gear and flap extension when only one engine is operating.

(5) Extend flaps to MANEUVER position at 140 mph.

(6) Reduce power carefully as needed.

(7) Neutralize rudder tab.

(8) Continue approach at not less than 120 mph.

(9) Do not extend full flaps until certain the airplane will make the field.

10) FURTHER INFORMATION.

(a) At rated power, 44″ Hg, 2600 rpm, the airplane will barely hold altitude with landing gear extended and flaps UP.

(b) With landing gear extended the airplane will not hold altitude at any flap extension.

(c) Things to avoid:

1. Extension of landing gear or flaps except when necessary for landing.

2. Accelerating throttle rapidly from reduced power to full power.

3. Low flat approaches with landing gear and flaps fully extended attempting to drag the airplane into the field with power. The technique should be developed to be always reducing power on the approach and avoid being forced to apply excessive power at low airspeeds.

e. TAKE-OFF IF LANDING IS NOT COMPLETED.

(1) Open throttles to take-off stop and after propeller rpm has stabilized, push propeller control forward to take-off position.

(2) Retract landing gear.

CAUTION

Pull the airplane up in a climb sufficient to stay below 150 mph indicated airspeed until the flaps are retracted.

(3) Retract flaps and proceed in normal take-off technique.

21. STOPPING ENGINES.

a. If a cold weather start is anticipated, the oil system should be diluted before stopping the engines. Idle the engines until oil temperature is below 70°C (158°F),
adjust the throttles to approximately 1000 rpm, hold the oil dilution switches (figure 5-2) ON for the required time as shown in chart below, pull the mixture controls (figure 4-6) to IDLE CUT-OFF, and release the oil dilution switches after the engines stop turning.

Oil Dilution Time in Minutes

Outside Air Temperatures	Dilution Minutes
4° to -12°C (40° to 10°F)	3
-12° to -29°C (10° to -20°F)	5
-29° to -46°C (-20° to -50°F)	8

b. If the oil temperature is above 40°C (104°F) upon completion of the diluting process, the engine should be shut down and allowed to cool until the oil temperature is below 40°C. The engine should then be restarted and the same diluting process repeated. This will avoid the possibility of evaporation of the fuel due to the high temperature nullifying the effect of the first dilution.

c. If oil dilution is not necessary, set the mixture controls to IDLE CUTOFF at 1200 rpm, and slowly move the throttles fully open.

d. After the engines stop turning, turn the ignition switches (figure 4-11) OFF and leave the mixture in CUTOFF.

22. BEFORE LEAVING PILOT'S COMPARTMENT.

a. Turn all switches and valves OFF.

b. Lock the controls.

(1) To set surface controls lock (figure 7-10), put rudders in neutral, push the right end of the locking tube forward of the guide angle (figure 7-4) and place the left end of the locking tube in the clip provided (figure 4-3). Strap control wheel to center of surface control lock. (Later airplanes are not equipped with rudder locks.)

c. Set the parking brake:

(1) Apply the toe brakes, pull the parking brake handle (figure 4-14) out and release the toe brakes.

CAUTION

Do not set the parking brake while the brake discs are hot.

23. TIEING DOWN.

a. This airplane is tied down by means of ropes which are passed through tie down lugs on each landing gear shock strut, or around the strut if lugs are not provided, and tied to stakes firmly anchored to the ground. Stakes and ropes are provided in the mooring kit which is stowed in the baggage compartment.

b. If extremely high wind conditions are encountered, additional ropes may be tied around the tail end of each boom and secured to some solid anchor point.

Flight Operating Data

1. AIRSPEED AND ALTIMETER CORRECTION TABLE.

Calibrated* I.A.S.	Airplane I.A.S. Gear and Flaps UP	Airplane I.A.S. Gear and Flaps DOWN	*ALTIMETER INSTALLATION ERRORS Gear and Flaps UP (feet)				
			Sea Level	10000	20000	30000	40000
100	83	89	+110	+130	+200	+270	+430
120	106	116	+100	+125	+195	+265	+420
140	130	140	+ 90	+115	+175	+250	+380
160	153	...	+ 70	+100	+140	+190	+300
180	176	...	+ 50	+ 60	+ 90	+130	+190
200	200	...	0	0	0	0	0
220	226	...	— 80	—110	—160	—230	...
240	248	...	—130	—170	—250	—330	...
260	269	...	—160	—230	—370	—430	...
280	291	...	—210	—290	—400	—550	...
300	312	...	—260	—360	—500	...	...
320	334	...	—325	—450	—620	...	...
340	356	...	—400	—540	—750	...	...
360	377	...	—500	—650	...	...	...

*Includes "Installation Errors" only. Does not include "Instrument Errors" as obtained by the Field Test Set.

+Add to altimeter reading
—Subtract from altimeter reading

SPECIFIC ENGINE
FLIGHT CHART

AIRPLANE MODELS

P-38H

ENGINE MODELS

V-1710-89 (RH)

V-1710-91 (LH)

CONDITION	FUEL PRESSURE (LB/SQ. IN.)	OIL PRESSURE (LB/SQ. IN.)	OIL TEMP. °C	OIL TEMP. °F	COOLANT TEMP. °C	COOLANT TEMP. °F
DESIRED	16–18	60–70	75–95	167–205	101–121	214–250
MAXIMUM	18	85	95	203	125	257
MINIMUM	12	55	40	104	85	185
IDLING	9	15				

MAX. PERMISSIBLE DIVING RPM: ....

CONDITION	ALLOWABLE OIL CONSUMPTION
NORMAL RATED (MAX. CONT.)	...13....U.S.QT/HR.......IMP.PT/HR
MAX. CRUISE	....9....U.S.QT/HR.......IMP.PT/HR
MIN. SPECIFIC	....7....U.S.QT/HR.......IMP.PT/HR

OIL GRADE: (S) .....1120.........**(W)**......1120 OR 1100.

SUPERCHARGER TYPE: EXHAUST DRIVEN TURBINE

FUEL GRADE: 100/130; SPEC. AN-F-28

OPERATING CONDITION	RPM	MANIFOLD PRESSURE (BOOST)	HORSE-POWER	CRITICAL ALTITUDE WITH RAM	CRITICAL ALTITUDE NO RAM	BLOWER	USE LOW BLOWER BELOW:	MIXTURE CONTROL POSITION	FUEL FLOW (GAL/HR/ENG.) U.S.	FUEL FLOW (GAL/HR/ENG.) IMP.	MAXIMUM CYL. TEMP. °C	MAXIMUM CYL. TEMP. °F	MAXIMUM DURATION (MINUTES)
TAKE-OFF	3000	54	1425		22,000**			AUTO-RICH	167				15
WAR EMERGENCY	3000	60	1600	10,000	7,000*			AUTO-RICH	180				5
MILITARY	3000	54	1425	24,900	22,000**			AUTO-RICH	167				15
NORMAL RATED (MAX. CONT.)	2600	44	1100	34,000	31,600**			AUTO-RICH	113				NO LIMIT
MAXIMUM CRUISE	2300	35	795	38,000	36,700**			AUTO-LEAN	63				NO LIMIT
MINIMUM SPECIFIC CONSUMPTION	2000 1700 1600 1600 1600	32 30 30 28 27	645 515 485 425 400	30,000 20,000 15,000 10,000 5,000				AUTO-LEAN	51 40 37 34 31				NO LIMIT

REMARKS: NEVER EXCEED THE FOLLOWING MANIFOLD PRESSURE AT THE ALTITUDE SHOWN REGARDLESS OF ENGINE R.P.M.

*WAR EMERGENCY POWER
**MILITARY POWER OR LESS

ALTITUDE	UP TO 10,000 CLIMB	UP TO 10,000 LEVEL FLIGHT	25,000 CLIMB	25,000 LEVEL FLIGHT	30,000 CLIMB	30,000 LEVEL FLIGHT	35,000 CLIMB	35,000 LEVEL FLIGHT	40,000 CLIMB	40,000 LEVEL FLIGHT
7,000	60	60	52	54	49	51	44	46	36	38
	54	54	52	54	48	51	41	43	33	34

FORM ASC-512A

SPECIFIC ENGINE
FLIGHT CHART

AIRPLANE MODELS

P-38J ....

F-5B ....

ENGINE MODELS

V-1710-89 (RH) ....

V-1710-91 (LH) ....

CONDITION	FUEL PRESSURE (LB/SQ. IN.)	OIL PRESSURE (LB/SQ. IN.)	OIL TEMP. °C	OIL TEMP. °F	COOLANT TEMP. °C	COOLANT TEMP. °F
DESIRED	16–18	60–70	75–95	167–203	101–121	214–250
MAXIMUM	18	85	95	203	125	257
MINIMUM	12	55	40	104	85	185
IDLING	9	15				

MAX. PERMISSIBLE DIVING RPM: ....

CONDITION	ALLOWABLE OIL CONSUMPTION	
NORMAL RATED (MAX. CONT.)	...13.... U.S.QT/HR	.... IMP.PT/HR
MAX. CRUISE	....9.... U.S.QT/HR	.... IMP.PT/HR
MIN. SPECIFIC	....7.... U.S.QT/HR	.... IMP.PT/HR

OIL GRADE: (S) .... 1120 .... **(W)** ... 1120 OR 1100 ...

SUPERCHARGER TYPE: EXHAUST DRIVEN TURBINE

FUEL GRADE: 100/130; SPEC. AN-F-28

OPERATING CONDITION	RPM	MANIFOLD PRESSURE (BOOST)	HORSE-POWER	CRITICAL ALTITUDE WITH RAM	CRITICAL ALTITUDE NO RAM	BLOWER	USE LOW BLOWER BELOW:	MIXTURE CONTROL POSITION	FUEL FLOW (GAL/HR/ENG.) U.S.	FUEL FLOW (GAL/HR/ENG.) IMP.	MAXIMUM CYL. TEMP. °C	MAXIMUM CYL. TEMP. °F	MAXIMUM DURATION (MINUTES)
TAKE-OFF	3000	54	1425		26,600**			AUTO-RICH	167				15 -
WAR EMERGENCY	3000	60	1600	28,700	25,800*			AUTO-RICH	180				5
MILITARY	3000	54	1425	29,000	26,600**			AUTO-RICH	167				15
NORMAL RATED (MAX. CONT.)	2600	44	1100	33,800	31,200**			AUTO-RICH	113				NO LIMIT
MAXIMUM CRUISE	2300	35	795	37,800	36,500**			AUTO-LEAN	63				NO LIMIT
MINIMUM SPECIFIC CONSUMPTION	2000 1700 1600 1600 1600	30 31 31 29 28	620 545 525 455 425	30,000 20,000 15,000 10,000 5,000				AUTO-LEAN	48 42 40 35 33				NO LIMIT

REMARKS: NEVER EXCEED THE FOLLOWING MANIFOLD PRESSURES AT THE ALTITUDE SHOWN REGARDLESS OF ENGINE R.P.M.

*WAR EMERGENCY POWER
**MILITARY POWER OR LESS

ALTITUDE	UP TO 26,000' CLIMB	UP TO 26,000' LEVEL FLIGHT	30,000 FT CLIMB	30,000 FT LEVEL FLIGHT	35,000 FT CLIMB	35,000 FT LEVEL FLIGHT	40,000 FT CLIMB	40,000 FT LEVEL FLIGHT
	60	60	53	57	45	48	37	39
	54	54	49	52	41	43	33	34

SPECIFIC ENGINE FLIGHT CHART

AIRPLANE MODELS

P-38L

ENGINE MODELS

V-1710-111 (R.H.)

V-1710-113 (L.H.)

CONDITION	FUEL PRESSURE (LB/SQ. IN.)	OIL PRESSURE (LB/SQ. IN.)	OIL TEMP. °C	OIL TEMP. °F	COOLANT TEMP. °C	COOLANT TEMP. °F
DESIRED	16–18	60–70	75–95	167–205	101–121	214–250
MAXIMUM	18	85	95	203	125	257
MINIMUM	12	55	40	104	85	185
IDLING	9	15				

MAX. PERMISSIBLE DIVING RPM: ....

CONDITION	ALLOWABLE OIL CONSUMPTION
NORMAL RATED (MAX. CONT.)	...13....U.S.QT/HR.......IMP.PT/HR
MAX. CRUISE	....9....U.S.QT/HR.......IMP.PT/HR
MIN. SPECIFIC	....7....U.S.QT/HR.......IMP.PT/HR

OIL GRADE: (S).....1120..........(W)....1120. OR .1100..

SUPERCHARGER TYPE: EXHAUST DRIVEN TURBINE

FUEL GRADE: 100/130; SPEC. AN-F-28

OPERATING CONDITION	RPM	MANIFOLD PRESSURE (BOOST)	HORSE-POWER	CRITICAL ALTITUDE WITH RAM	CRITICAL ALTITUDE NO RAM	BLOWER	USE LOW BLOWER BELOW:	MIXTURE CONTROL POSITION	FUEL FLOW (GAL/HR/ENG.) U.S.	FUEL FLOW (GAL/HR/ENG.) IMP.	MAXIMUM CYL. TEMP. °C	MAXIMUM CYL. TEMP. °F	MAXIMUM DURATION (MINUTES)
TAKE-OFF	3000	54	1425		26,600**			AUTO-RICH	167				15
WAR EMERGENCY	3000	60	1600	28,700	25,800*			AUTO-RICH	180				5
MILITARY	3000	54	1425	29,000	26,600**			AUTO-RICH	167				15
NORMAL RATED (MAX. CONT.)	2600	44	1100	33,800	31,200**			AUTO-RICH	113				NO LIMIT
MAXIMUM CRUISE	2300	35	795	37,800	36,500**			AUTO-LEAN	63				NO LIMIT
MINIMUM SPECIFIC CONSUMPTION	2000 / 1700 / 1600 / 1600 / 1600	30 / 31 / 31 / 29 / 28	620 / 545 / 525 / 455 / 425	30,000 / 20,000 / 15,000 / 10,000 / 5,000				AUTO-LEAN	48 / 42 / 40 / 35 / 33				NO LIMIT

REMARKS: NEVER EXCEED THE FOLLOWING MANIFOLD PRESSURES AT THE ALTITUDE SHOWN REGARDLESS OF ENGINE R.P.M.

*WAR EMERGENCY POWER
**MILITARY POWER OR LESS

ALTITUDE	UP TO 26,000' CLIMB	UP TO 26,000' LEVEL FLIGHT	30,000 FT. CLIMB	30,000 FT. LEVEL FLIGHT	35,000 FT. CLIMB	35,000 FT. LEVEL FLIGHT	40,000 FT. CLIMB	40,000 FT. LEVEL FLIGHT
	60	60	53	57	45	48	37	39
	54	.54	49	52	41	43	33	34

OPERATING LIMITS USING GRADE 91 FUEL

NOTE—USE GRADE 91 FUEL ONLY IF MODIFICATIONS ACCORDING TO TO-02-5A-66 HAVE BEEN COMPLIED WITH.

AIRPLANE MODELS: P-38H P-38J P-38L F-5B

ENGINE MODELS: V-1710-89 V-1710-91 V-1710-111 V-1710-113

FUEL: GRADE 91/96   SPEC. AN-F-26

OPERATING CONDITIONS	MANIFOLD PRESSURE (Max. In. Hg)	R. P. M. (Max.)	HORSE POWER	MIXTURE CONTROL POSITION	BLOWER	MAXIMUM DURATION (Min.)
TAKE-OFF	47	3000	1325	AUTO RICH	SEA LEVEL	5
	40	3000	1098	AUTO RICH	25,000 FT. ALTITUDE	5
NORMAL RATED	38	2600	1000	AUTO RICH		NO LIMIT
MAXIMUM CRUISING	32	2300	755	AUTO RICH		NO LIMIT
DESIRED CRUISING	28	2200	605	AUTO LEAN		NO LIMIT

REMARKS: 1. Reduce above manifold pressures 2″ Hg for each 5°C (9°F) above 43°C (110°F) carburetor air temperature.
2. Reduce above manifold pressures 2″ Hg for each 1,000 ft. above 27,000 ft. until 20″ Hg is reached.

Emergency Operating Instructions

1. ENGINE FAILURE DURING FLIGHT.

a. FAILURE OF ONE ENGINE.

(1) PERFORMANCE.—The airplane flies well on one engine. Using normal rated power, it will climb to about 26,500 feet, and can be flown at more than 255 mph (true speed) in level flight at 20,000 feet.

(2) FEATHERING EMERGENCY.

(a) Reduce the power from the live engine if necessary to maintain directional control. This should not be necessary if the indicated airspeed is 125 mph or more.

(b) Apply all the power to the good engine that can be held, preventing yaw at all times.

(c) Hold 125 mph or more (at least 160 mph preferred).

(d) Release droppable fuel tanks, bombs, or chemical tanks, immediately.

(e) Trim rudder tab slowly to take pressure off rudder pedal.

(f) Carefully move mixture control of bad engine to IDLE CUT-OFF.

(g) Carefully select propeller feathering switch (figure 4-13) of bad engine and feather propeller.

WARNING

If the propeller does not feather, then attempt to feather it by holding the selector switch (figure 4-5) in the DEC RPM position. If the propeller still will not feather then it is desirable to fly at a low airspeed (130 to 140 mph) to keep the propeller windmilling at the lowest possible rpm.

(h) Turn off electric fuel pump switch and fuel tank selector valve control of failed engine.

(i) Close coolant and oil cooler scoops of failed engine.

(j) If the left engine has failed, and consequently the generator has stopped, take action indicated under ELECTRICAL FAILURE, Section IV, paragraph 10. (This is not applicable to F-5B, P-38L, and late P-38J airplanes which have a generator on each engine.)

(k) Climb to safe altitude and reduce power to maintain 160 mph indicated airspeed.

(l) Return to field and fly around until familiar with airplane's behavior on single engine.

(3) SINGLE ENGINE APPROACH AND LANDING.

CAUTION

Concentrate sharply on your approach—because once you have fully extended the flaps, and the landing gear or descended below 500 feet, you cannot again circle the field and you must make a landing. If, however, the flaps are not fully extended and your elevation is still 500 feet or more, and you want to go around again, proceed as follows before beginning to circle:

(1) Apply as much power as can be held, at the same time retracting the landing gear,

(2) Accelerate to at least 160 MPH, and

(3) Raise the flaps.

It is recommended that the inexperienced pilot practice single engine landing by completely closing one throttle and setting the corresponding propeller lever to the "DECREASE RPM" (full rear) position. With this procedure the throttled engine will present nearly the same drag as a feathered propeller and if necessary both throttles may be opened to go around. Don't forget to push the propeller levers forward if it is necessary to go around.

Note

TURNS CAN BE MADE SAFELY IN EITHER DIRECTION AS LONG AS AIRSPEED IS HELD CONSTANT ABOVE CRITICAL SINGLE ENGINE SPEED, AND AIRPLANE IS PROPERLY TRIMMED.

(a) Secure radio clearance for emergency landing.

(b) Turn aileron control booster OFF to conserve hydraulic power for landing gear and flap operation.

(c) Start approach allowing 1000 feet above field for each two miles away.

(d) Extend landing gear at 160 mph.

Note

Allow more time for landing gear and flap extension when only one engine is operating.

(e) Extend flaps to MANEUVER position at 140 mph.

(f) Reduce power carefully as needed.

(g) Neutralize rudder tab.

(h) Continue approach at not less than 120 mph.

(i) Do not extend full flaps until certain the airplane will make the field.

(4) FURTHER INFORMATION.

(a) At rated power, 44" Hg. 2600 rpm, the airplane will barely hold altitude with landing gear extended and flaps up.

(b) With landing gear extended the airplane will not hold altitude at any flap extension.

(c) Things to avoid:

1. Extension of landing gear or flaps except when necessary for landing.

2. Accelerating throttle rapidly from reduced power to full power.

3. Low flat approaches with landing gear and flaps fully extended attempting to drag the airplane into the field with power. The technique should be developed to be always reducing power on the approach and avoid being forced to apply excessive power at low airspeeds.

(5) FEATHERING—PRACTICE.

(a) Close throttle.

(b) Mixture—IDLE CUT-OFF.

(c) Move propeller feathering switch to feathering position.

CAUTION

On all airplanes, except F-5B, P-38L and late P-38J airplanes which have a generator on each engine, shut down the right-hand engine so that the generator which is on the left engine will remain in operation.

(6) UNFEATHERING IN FLIGHT.

(a) Propeller control (figure 4-4) DEC RPM (full rearward).

(b) Throttle 1/10 to 1/4 open.

(c) Return propeller feathering switch to NORMAL position.

(d) Lift the guard on the propeller selector switch of the feathered propeller.

Note

It is recommended that the above operations be performed immediately after feathering is completed so that the engine may be started quickly in case the live engine should fail during practice.

(e) Hold the propeller selector switch (figure 4-5) in INC RPM until the engine is turning 600 to 800 rpm then place it in AUTO CONSTANT SPEED. Place mixture control in AUTO RICH. The engine should start.

(f) Warm up the engine before operating at full power.

b. FAILURE OF BOTH ENGINES.

(1) Drop external tanks or bombs.

(2) Turn fuel selector valves OFF.

(3) Set mixture controls to IDLE CUTOFF.

(4) Turn ignition OFF.

(5) Turn battery switch OFF.

(6) Release the cockpit canopy and roll down both side windows.

(7) Extend flaps by use of hand pump if there is sufficient time.

(8) Leave the landing gear up.

(9) Make a normal approach at 8 or 10 mph over the stalling speed and set the airplane on the ground slightly before the stall is reached.

2. FIRE.

a. There are no fire extinguishers installed in this airplane. If an engine fire occurs, shut off tank selector valve to that engine, turn boost pump OFF, and move mixture control to IDLE CUTOFF.

3. EMERGENCY EXIT.

a. RECOMMENDED METHOD. — Slow down as much as possible, (below 200 mph) and trim the airplane in an approximately level attitude. If time permits head airplane towards an unpopulated area. Pull the emergency hatch release control (figure 23-4) to release the top hatch, crank or push either side window down, crawl out and slide off the wing head first.

b. ALTERNATE METHOD. — If it is still possible to control the airplane, turn the airplane upside down, unhook the safety belt, and fall out.

4. DROPPABLE FUEL TANK OR BOMB EMERGENCY RELEASE.

a. A droppable tank or bomb emergency release is installed in later airplanes. It is located either behind and to the left of the pilot's seat or directly in front of the pilot's seat.

5. EMERGENCY WING FLAP OPERATION.

a. If the pressure from the engine driven hydraulic pump fails to extend the flaps, they may be extended as follows:

(1) Turn coolant override switches (figure 5-13) OFF.

(2) Turn the aileron boost shutoff valve (figure 9-5) OFF.

(3) Move flap control (figure 7-2) to MANEUVER or DOWN.

(4) Turn source selector valve handle (figure 17-4) to UP. (This is the normal position.)

(5) Operate the hand pump (figure 17-2) until the desired flap extension is obtained.

b. If the above system fails to extend the flaps, leave the control at DOWN while extending the landing gear. Oil from the return side of the landing gear cylinders may fill the system enough to cause the flaps to operate.

Note

The auxiliary system should be used for flap extension because in some cases there may not be sufficient fluid to extend both landing gear and flaps, and the landing gear may be extended with the emergency system fluid.

CAUTION

If one engine has failed in addition to the hydraulic system failure, remember that the airplane cannot maintain level flight on one engine with landing gear and flaps extended. Under these conditions it may be desirable to land with flaps UP.

6. EMERGENCY LANDING GEAR OPERATION.

a. Check to see that the coolant override switches and the aileron booster shut-off valve are in the OFF position. Place all controls in the normal position for landing gear extension and operate the hand pump (figure 17-2).

Note

Nose gear door must open and nose gear must unlock before any pressure will flow to the main gear door cylinders.

b. If, after considerable pumping, no reading is given on the position indicator operate the emergency system as follows:

(1) Source-selector valve handle; (figure 17-4) break safety wire and push DOWN.

(2) Bypass valve (figure 17-3); break safety wire and CLOSE tightly. (On later airplanes, the bypass valve is controlled by the source selector valve control. If bypass valve is not provided, disregard operation (2).)

(3) Check landing gear control DOWN and operate the hand pump while yawing the airplane from side to side.

Note

This system opens the landing gear doors by forcing them with the wheels.

7. EMERGENCY LANDING WITH WHEELS RETRACTED.

a. When a belly landing is necessary, it should be made without external tanks. Use 1/2 to full flaps.

Note

When imminent belly landing is due to apparent hydraulic failure, unless forced down by lack of fuel or approaching darkness, don't give up until all methods of landing gear extension have been tried thoroughly and exhaustively.

b. Make a normal approach at 8 or 10 mph over the stalling speed and set the airplane on the ground slightly before the stall is reached. Set the mixture control to CUTOFF and turn the battery switch OFF before contact.

8. EMERGENCY LANDING IN WATER (DITCHING).

a. Unless the water is very smooth, it will probably be more desirable to bail out of the airplane than to try to land it on the water.

b. If a water landing is necessary, preparations for abandoning the airplane should be made while still in the air. Release bombs or droppable tanks and the top hatch, and push down both side windows. Leave the shoulder harness on to prevent the shock of landing from throwing the head forward into the bullet-proof glass and the gunsight.

(1) Since a much flatter approach can be made with power on, the landing should be made before the fuel has been completely used up.

(2) Wind and surface conditions should be noted so that the approach may be made along the swell and as near into the wind as possible.

c. Make contact with landing gear and flaps UP, (water landings with gear down are invariably fatal) and at an airspeed slightly above the stalling point.

d. After landing, release the safety belt and swim clear of the airplane before it sinks. The airplane can not be expected to stay afloat once it comes to rest. The seat back cushion provided with the airplane is also a life preserver.

9. ICING CONDITIONS.

a. Pitot heat (figure 5-14) ON.

b. The formation of carburetor ice is unlikely due to the injection type carburetors and the heating effect of the turbo-superchargers. It is possible, however, that ice could form while flying at low powers in a humid atmosphere.

c. If icing conditions are present during a landing approach, move the throttles occasionally to prevent ice from freezing them in a closed position. Extend landing gear, lower flaps to maneuvering position, and make the approach under partial power.

d. If carburetor ice forms in cruising flight, it may be removed by increasing the power boldly and putting the airplane into a steep climb. Intercooler shutters (on P-38J, P-38L and F-5B airplanes only) should be closed as far as possible without exceeding the maximum 45°C (113°F) carburetor air temperature.

e. Ice formation on the windshield may be removed by turning the cockpit heat ON and directing the flexible heater tube to the desired point on the glass.

10. ELECTRICAL FAILURE.

a. Electrical failure may be indicated by a zero reading on the voltmeter (figure 5-8) and the ammeter (figure 8-12) and by rapidly diminishing battery power (the first indication of a low battery will be given by failure of the propeller governors to hold the proper rpm). When the above conditions are noticed:

(1) Set the propeller selector switches to FIXED PITCH.

(2) Set the oil cooler flap switches to OFF.

(3) Restrict the use of all lights and radio.

(4) If practicable, turn the battery switch OFF until electrical power is needed.

(5) If it is necessary to land with the propeller selector switches on MANUAL, the following setting should be made to insure that sufficient power will be available and that the engines will not overspeed in the event of mislanding. Make this adjustment, if possible, while there is still sufficient battery power to operate the propellers.

(a) Altitude—Not over 5,000 feet above the airport.

(b) Adjust the throttles and propeller selector switches to obtain 2600 rpm and 25" Hg. manifold pressure at an approximate airspeed of 180 mph in level flight.

Operational Equipment

1. HEATING AND VENTILATING.

a. COCKPIT HEAT.—Cockpit heat is supplied by an intensifier tube in the right engine exhaust (both engines on late airplanes) and controlled by a knob (figure 7-3) on the windshield support. Heat outlets are arranged to supply warm air to the windshield and removable hatch. The foot heat outlet may be closed off by operating the heat control (figure 26-5) on the floor under the right foot. On later airplanes, a heated flying suit plug and rheostat are located on the left side of the cockpit.

b. VENTILATING AIR.—Ventilating air enters from the left wing fuselage fillet. The rate of flow may be varied by rotating the ventilator (figure 4-30) as desired.

c. ARMAMENT OR CAMERA COMPARTMENT HEAT.—Armament or camera compartment heat is supplied by an intensifier tube in the left engine exhaust on early airplanes. The heat control (figure 4-23) on the left windshield support is used to turn the heat ON and OFF. On late airplanes the left engine heat has been diverted to the cockpit. Electric gun heaters are used on these airplanes and are turned on by a switch on the main switch box.

2. OXYGEN SYSTEM.

a. Full pressure in the three oxygen bottles is 400 to 450 lb/sq in.

Altitude 1,000 Feet	Hours of Supply		Auto Mix—OFF
	Auto Mix—ON *		
0	8.8		1.6
5	8.3	**	1.9
10	11.0	14.1	2.2
15	11.0	8.1	2.9
20	11.2	7.0	3.7
25	6.3	6.1	4.6
30	6.4	6.4	6.1
35	8.4	8.4	8.4
40	12.0	12.0	12.0

* Pioneer regulator
** Air Reduction Sales Regulator

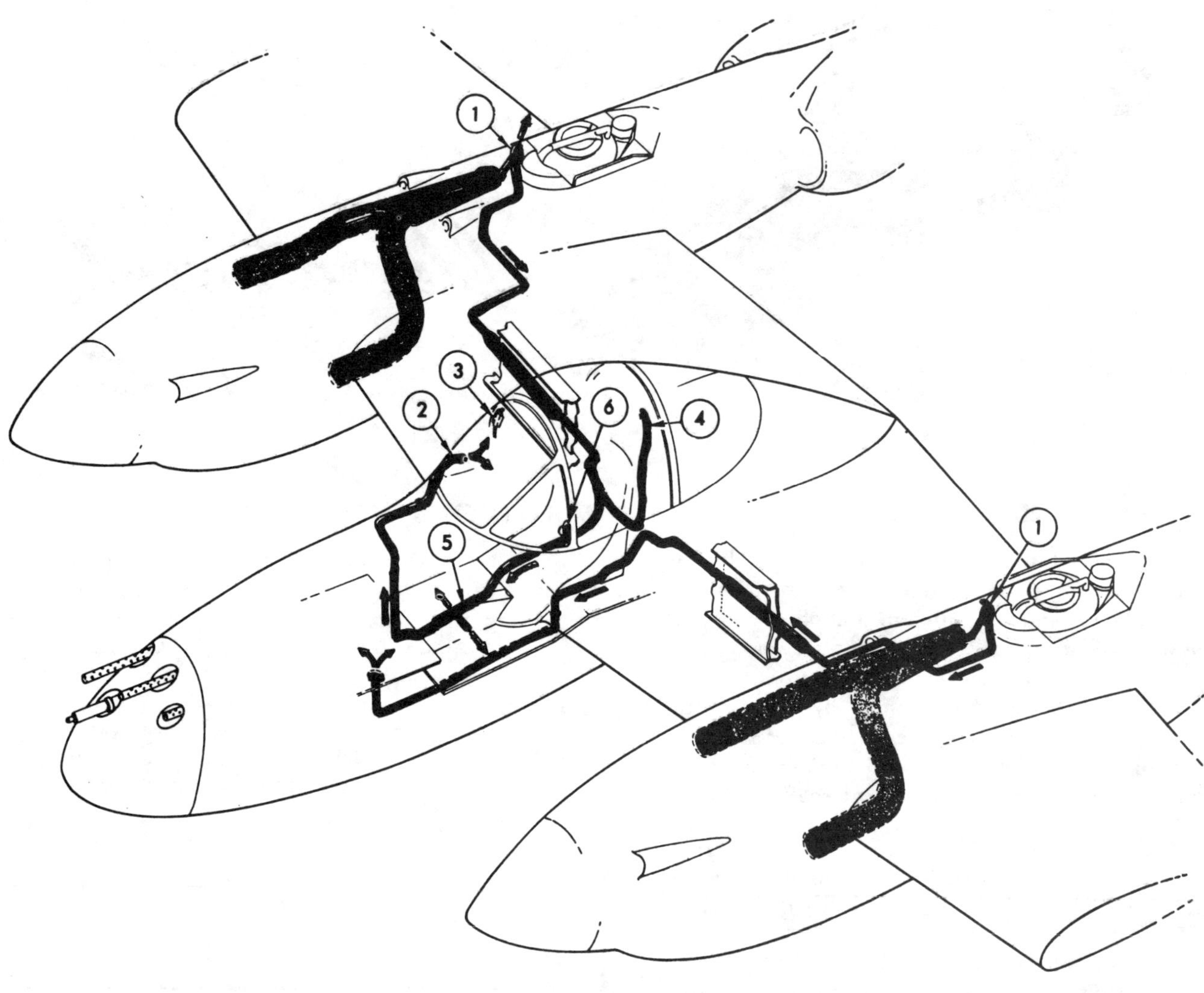

Exhaust Manifold

Cockpit Heat Lines

Armament Heat Lines
(Diverted to cockpit on
late airplanes)

1. Heat by-pass (shut-off) valves. (2)

2. Windshield defroster tube.

3. Cockpit heat control.

4. Flexible hatch defroster tube.

5. Foot heat shut-off valve.

6. Gun (or camera) heat control.
   (Cockpit heat control on late airplanes.)

Figure 26 — Heating System Diagram

b. Fit the demand-type mask snugly to the face and test the fit by pinching the tube and sucking lightly. The mask should collapse. Clip the mask tube to the clothing allowing for all necessary head movement without pulling the mask away from the face.

WARNING

It must be remembered that the suction of breathing is used to open the oxygen valve, and that any leakage in the mask will cause this valve to become inoperative and will stop the flow of oxygen.

(c) Make certain the knurled collar at the outlet end of the regulator is tight. Examine top diaphragm to see that it is not ruptured or distorted.

(d) Turn emergency knob (Figure 27-4) "ON" to check the flow. Check the pressure gage to see that there is no perceptible pressure drop. Turn emergency knob "OFF" and ascertain that it does not leak. Leave it in this position.

(e) Turn the auto-mix (Figure 27-3) to "OFF". Note on flow indicator (Figure 27-1) that on inhalation the top diaphragm goes down and that nearly 100 percent oxygen is received. Turn the auto-mix to "ON" and note that there is little or no indication of oxygen flow on the indicator. Leave in this position.

(f) Check pressure of the system. It must not be less than 365 lbs./sq.in. Before take-off, make certain that the pressure gage (Figure 4-34) shows sufficient oxygen

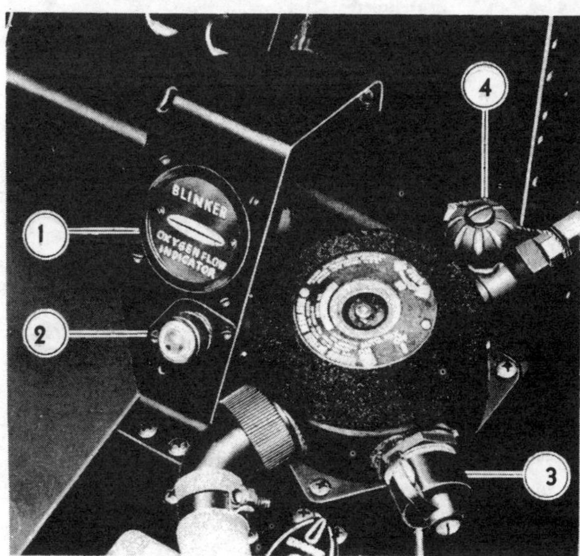

1. Oxygen flow indicator
2. Oxygen pressure warning light.
3. Auto-mix lever.
4. Emergency knob.

Figure 27 — Oxygen Controls

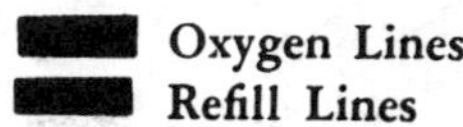

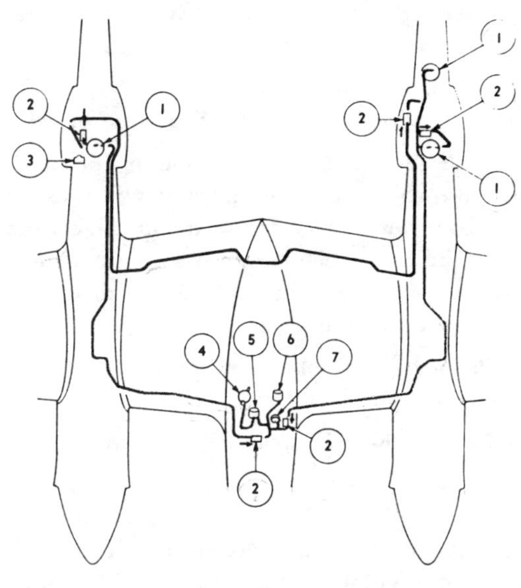

1. Oxygen bottles.
2. Check valves.
3. Refill connection.
4. Demand type oxygen regulator.
5. Oxygen flowmeter.
6. Oxygen pressure gage.
7. Pressure warning light.

Figure 28 — Oxygen System Diagram

supply for the mission. The oxygen pressure warning unit (Figure 27-2) indicates when the pressure drops below approximately 100 lbs./sq.in.

(g) With the auto-mix and the emergency controls both turned OFF, pure oxygen will be supplied as required by normal breathing. This setting, however, is wasteful of oxygen and should be used only in an emergency, when denitrogenizing for high altitude flight has been accomplished, or during night flights for improved vision.

3. COMMUNICATIONS EQUIPMENT.

a. These airplanes may be equipped with an SCR-522 command set as shown in figure 7 or an SCR-274N command set illustrated in figure 29. An SCR-695-A radio and a Detrola model 438 beacon receiver have been provided. Provisions are made for the installation of a BC-608 contactor.

b. OPERATION OF THE SCR-522 RADIO.

(1) Plug the headphones and microphones into the jack (figure 17-5).

(2) Check the generator switch (figure 5-16 or 8-11) and the battery switch (figure 5-15) ON.

(3) Set the selector switch (figure 7-9) to REM. The T and R positions of this switch are not to be used.

(4) Push the A, B, C, or D button (figure 7-7), depending on which pre-tuned frequency is to be used, and wait about one minute for warm-up. Lights beside each button indicate which button has been pushed. The lever (figure 7-6) beside the OFF button may be used to dim the indicator lights.

(5) Press the microphone button and speak slowly and clearly.

(6) Release the microphone button to receive.

Note

The T and R positions are provided for use on installations employing a separate radio operator. Transmission is impossible with the switch in the R position; reception is impossible with the switch in the T position. The lock lever (figure 7-8) spring loads the selector switch to the R position and prevents operation in the REM position.

(7) To turn off the equipment, push the OFF button (figure 7-5).

Note

This radio is not equipped with a volume control. Most installations have a remote volume control installed on the junction box on the right hand side of the cockpit over the hydraulic hand pump.

c. OPERATION OF THE SCR-274N RADIO.— There are three separate receivers, and any two of four available transmitters may be installed.

Receiver Frequencies	Transmitter Frequencies
190 to 550 kilocycles	3 to 4 megacycles
3 to 6 megacycles	4.0 to 5.3 megacycles
6 to 9.1 megacycles	5.3 to 7.0 megacycles
	7.0 to 9.1 megacycles

The receivers may be tuned in flight; the transmitters are pre-tuned to the proper frequency on the ground.

(1) RECEIVING.

(a) Plug the headphones into the jack JK-26 (figure 29-14) which is, in turn, plugged into the bottom of the filter box (figure 29-9).

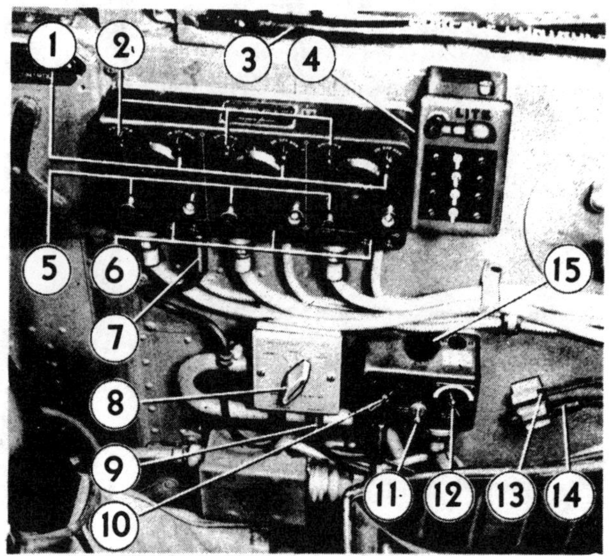

1. Main power switch (receivers).
2. Headset selector switches.
3. Surface controls lock.
4. Recognition light switch box.
5. Volume controls.
6. Tuning cranks.
7. Tel. plug (in B jack).
8. Radio range filter switch.
9. Headset jack.
10. Emission selector switch.
11. Main power switch (transmitter).
12. Transmitter selector switch.
13. Microphone jack (stowed).
14. Headset extension cord jack (stowed).
15. Transmitter key.

Figure 29 — SCR 274N Radio Controls

(b) Determine the frequency to be used and turn the main power switch (figure 29-1) for that receiver to MCW or to CW, depending on the type of reception desired.

(c) For normal reception, set the range selector switch (figure 29-8) to BOTH. To receive radio range without voice interference, set the selector switch to RANGE. To eliminate radio range interference from a station broadcasting range and voice signals on the same frequency, set the selector switch to VOICE.

(d) Note which jack (A or B) the TEL plug (figure 29-7) is in and turn the headset selector switch (figure 29-2) of the receiver being used to corresponding position (A or B).

(e) Adjust the volume (figure 29-5) to obtain a light frying noise and tune in the desired station using the crank (figure 29-6).

Note

Two or three receivers may be turned on simultaneously by following the instructions contained in paragraphs *(d)* and *(e)* above for each receiver.

(2) TRANSMITTING.

(a) Select the desired frequency with the transmitter selector switch (figure 29-12).

(b) Plug the microphone into the jack JK-48 (figure 29-13) which is plugged into the bottom of the transmitter control box.

(c) Turn the main power switch (figure 29-11) ON and allow 15 seconds for the transmitter to warm up.

(d) Turn the emission selector (figure 29-10) to CW, MCW, or TONE as desired.

(e) If MCW was selected, press the microphone button and talk slowly and clearly.

(f) If CW or TONE is selected, operate the key (figure 29-15).

d. DETROLA MODEL 438 BEACON RECEIVER.— This receiver is in addition to the SCR-522 or the SCR-274N radio when the airplane leaves the factory. If it is still installed:

(1) Plug headphones into the jack (figure 17-5) which is plugged into the face of the radio panel.

(2) Turn the volume control (figure 7-15) up until the background noise is heard.

(3) Tune to the desired frequency with the tuning knob (figure 7-14).

(4) Frequencies covered are 200 to 400 kilocycles.

e. SCR-695-A RADIO.

(1) Before take-off insert the destructor plug in the radio located just forward of, and accessible through the baggage compartment door on the right boom. The destructor plug socket is on the right side, set apart from the group of three sockets on the left side of the radio.

DANGER

Do not insert the destructor plug if the red warning lights, located over the radio set in the boom, are lighted. Make sure that the warning light system has been checked and is in proper working order.

(2) After take-off set the "ON-OFF" switch (figure 30-3) to "ON".

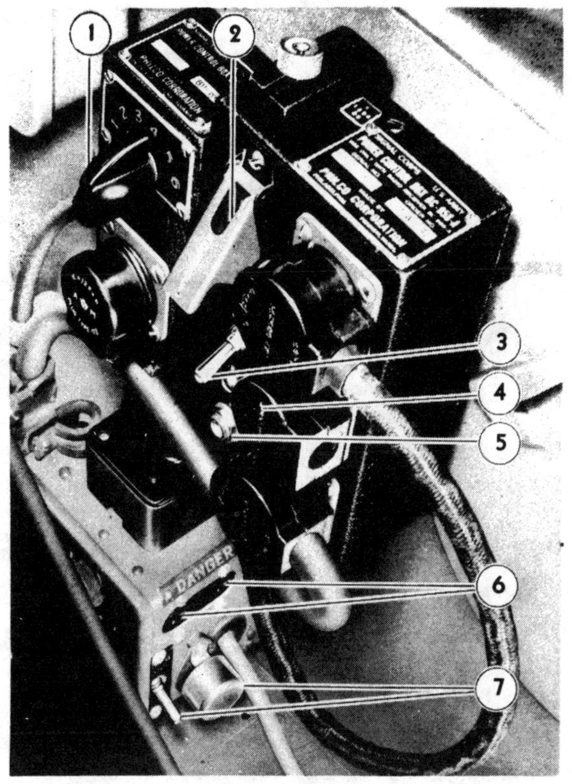

1. Six-position switch.
2. Emergency switch.
3. ON-OFF switch.
4. Protection plug (to prevent short circuit with safety belt).
5. Headset jack.
6. Destructor buttons.
7. "G" band switches.

Figure 30 — SCR 695-A Radio Controls

(3) Set the six-position switch (figure 30-1) to the position specified by the Communications Officer-in-Charge. (In the absence of specific information, set to "1".)

(4) Set the "G" band switches (figure 30-7) as directed by the Communications Officer.

(5) Details concerning the use of the EMERGENCY switch (figure 30-2) and destructor buttons (figure 30-6) should be obtained from the Communications Officer.

(6) To stop the equipment, turn all switches OFF.

(7) Disconnect the destructor plug as soon as the airplane lands in friendly territory.

f. BC-608 CONTACTOR. — Provisions have been made for the installation of this unit when in British squadrons or when operating in conjunction with British airplanes.

(1) Before take-off, turn the contactor heater switch ON, wind the clock and synchronize it with the control clock by setting the clock switch (figure 31-3) to RUN at the given signal.

(2) Turn the command transmitter ON.

(3) Turn the contactor switch (figure 31-1) to IN.

(a) Automatic transmission takes place during the 15 seconds the clock hand is between the 12:00 and the 3:00 o'clock position. Normal transmission and reception is not possible during this time.

g. MN-26Y RADIO COMPASS.—This radio compass may be installed in some airplanes. The compass is intended for use during the ferry flights, and may be removed in combat zones.

(1) GENERAL.

(a) The master control switch marked OFF, COMP., REC. ANT., and REC. LOOP controls all radio compass equipment functions other than tuning and adjustment of signal level.

(b) The COMP setting is used for obtaining communications reception, visual on-course indication of homing and bearings.

(c) The REC. ANT setting is used for communication and aural radio range reception.

(d) The REC. LOOP setting is used for obtaining communications reception during conditions of severe rain and snow static, aural radio range reception, aural null homing from communication stations.

(e) The OFF setting opens all current consuming circuits thus rendering the equipment inoperative.

(f) The left-right indicator indicates whether the station is to the right or left of the centerline of the airplane.

(2) OPERATION OF THE MN-26Y RADIO COMPASS.

(a) Turn the main switch ON and set the band selector switch to the frequency range desired.

(b) Tune to the desired station and adjust the volume (audio) control. Set the CW switch to ON for code reception, OFF for voice reception.

(c) Set the master switch according to the operation to be conducted.

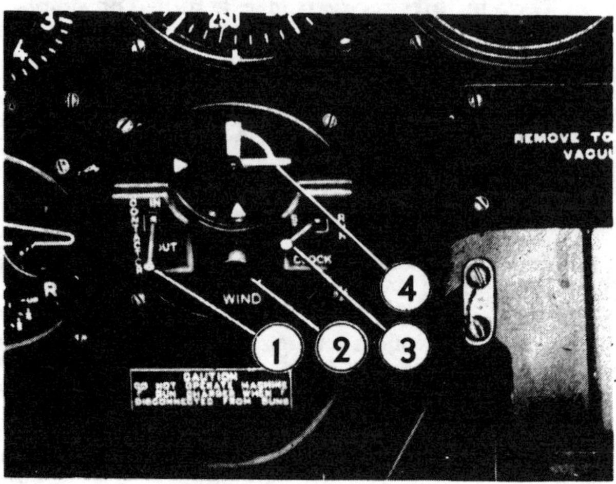

1. Contactor in-out switch.
2. Clock winding knob.
3. Clock stop-run switch.
4. Clock indicator.

Figure 31 — BC 608 Contactor Controls

4. ARMAMENT.

a. The P-38H, P-38J and P-38L airplanes are equipped with four, .50 caliber machine guns and one 20 mm cannon and a small motion picture camera. Space is provided for carrying 500 rounds of ammunition for each .50 caliber gun and 150 rounds for the 20 mm cannon. The motion picture camera operates with the guns to record results.

(1) Before take-off check that machine guns and cannon have been charged. (P-38H airplanes only are equipped with a machine gun charger which may be operated in flight as follows:)

(a) Pull the charging selector (figure 4-16) out and turn it to the gun to be charged.

(b) Pull the charging handle (figure 4-10) all the way back and then push it forward.

(c) Strike the charging selector with the heel of the hand.

Note

Never attempt to move the charging selector unless the charging handle is in the full forward position.

(d) Charge the other three machine guns in the same manner.

(2) Turn the armament switch (on control column) to COMBAT.

(3) Push the machine gun button or the cannon button (on control wheel) to fire the guns.

(a) If it is desired to use the camera without the guns, set the armament switch to CAMERA and operate either the gun or cannon button.

Note

Turn gun heat (figure 4-23, or switch on main switch box) ON whenever the outside air temperature is below freezing.

(4) The optical gun sight is turned ON by the rheostat (figure 5-10) which adjusts the intensity of the reflection on the glass behind the windshield. Adjust the seat vertically until the sight reflection is easily visible.

(5) When flying in bright sunlight, place the dark glass (figure 4-31) in position over the gunsight (figure 32-2). Later airplanes are not equipped with gunsight dark glass.

(6) To drop bombs, set the arming switch (figure 4-24) to ARM (or safe), set the bomb selector switch (figure 4-20) to ON for the bomb to be dropped and, while flying at less than 400 mph I AS and not more than 30° from the horizontal, with flaps UP, press the release button (figure 4-27).

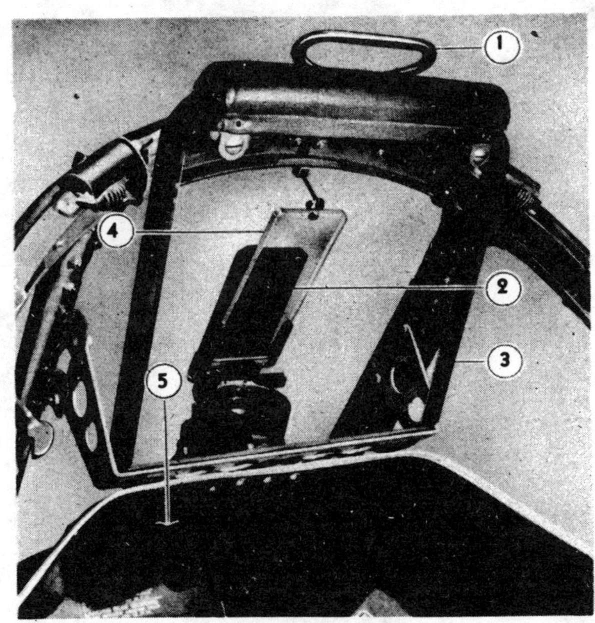

1. Emergency hatch release.
2. Gunsight dark glass.
3. Bullet proof glass.
4. Reflecting glass.
5. Glare shield.

Figure 32 — Gun Sight (Early Airplanes)

5. PHOTOGRAPHIC EQUIPMENT.

a. On F-5B airplanes all the cameras are installed in the fuselage nose which is divided into three camera compartments. The forward compartment accommodates one 6-inch K-17 chart camera. The center compartment will accommodate two 6-inch K-17 chart cameras or one 12-inch or 24-inch K-17 reconnaissance camera. The aft compartment accommodates two 24-inch K-17, or one 24-inch K-18, reconnaissance cameras.

b. CAMERA OPERATION.

(1) Before take-off the pilot should determine which cameras are installed and that the airplane is properly balanced. THIS IS IMPORTANT (see Section II, paragraph 2, *a.*

(2) TO OPERATE CAMERAS:

(a) Set camera diaphragm control (figure 33-4) as required. (Bright, medium, or cloudy.)

(b) Turn camera switches (figures 33-6, 7 or 8) ON for each group of cameras to be used.

Note

Camera heat (figure 4-23) should be adjusted to maintain approximately 5°C (40°F) on the camera compartment temperature indicator (figure 33-1). Some airplanes may be equipped with ethylene glycol electric fan heaters which will be operated through a switch and rheostat in the cockpit.

(c) FOR INTERVALOMETER OPERATION:

1. Determine time interval from the INTERVALOMETER SETTING table (figure 34).

2. Set the intervalometer hand to the selected time interval. Push and turn knob (figure 33-11) to set hand.

3. Set the camera control switch (figure 33-9) to INTERVALOMETER.

4. Turn camera master switch (figure 33-5) ON. An exposure will be made immediately.

5. Amber lights flash when exposure is made. Green lights indicate when film is winding. The white light gives a three-second warning before exposure.

6. To take an extra picture at any instant, set the control switch to RUNAWAY and immediately return it to INTERVALOMETER.

(d) FOR MANUAL CONTROL:

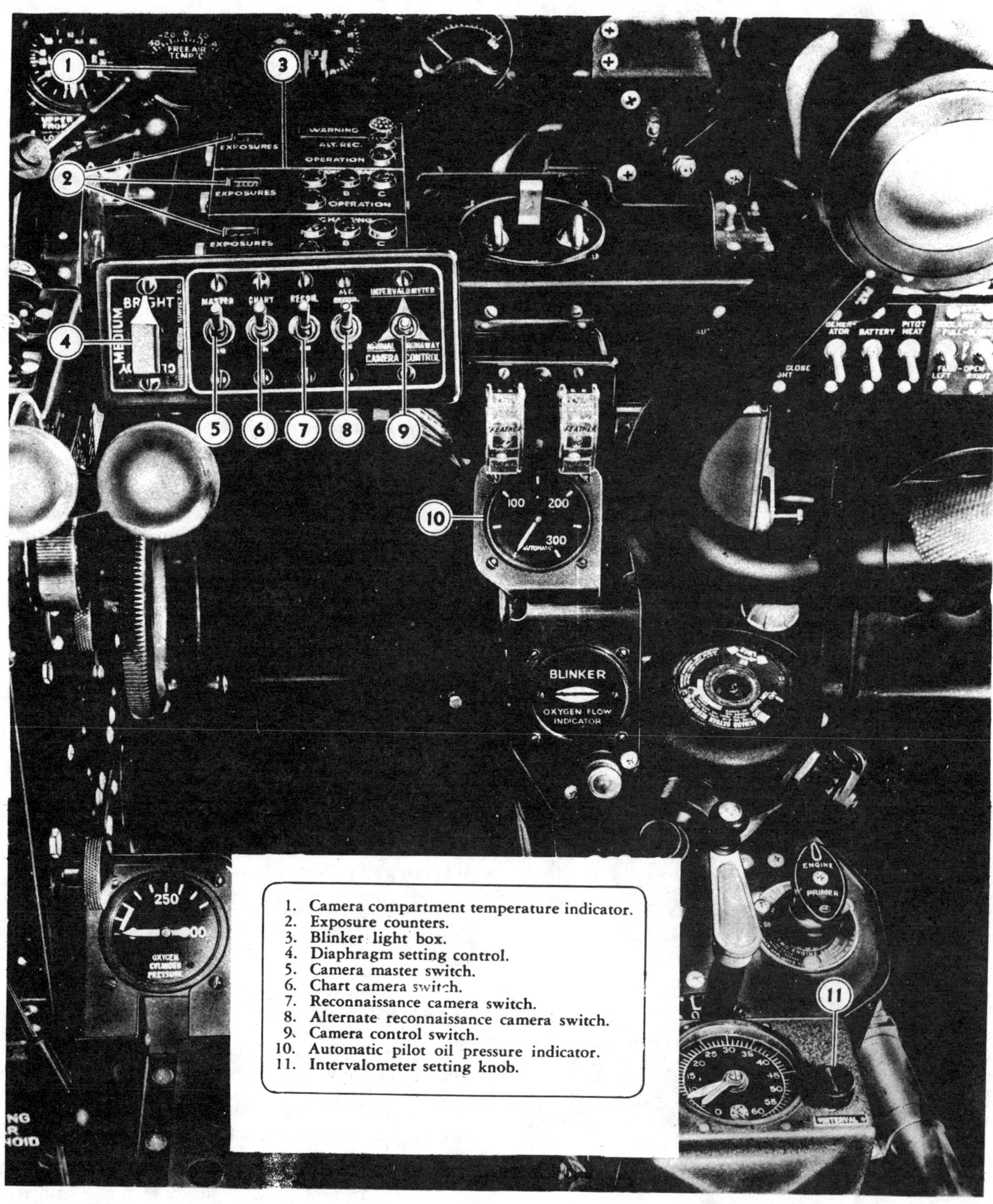

1. Camera compartment temperature indicator.
2. Exposure counters.
3. Blinker light box.
4. Diaphragm setting control.
5. Camera master switch.
6. Chart camera switch.
7. Reconnaissance camera switch.
8. Alternate reconnaissance camera switch.
9. Camera control switch.
10. Automatic pilot oil pressure indicator.
11. Intervalometer setting knob.

Figure 33 — A-1 Camera Controls

(F-5B ONLY)

1. Set camera control switch to MANUAL.

2. Turn camera master switch ON.

3. Pull the camera control trigger, (on the control wheel) to make an exposure.

(e) FOR RUNAWAY OPERATION:

1. Set camera control switch to RUNAWAY.

2. Turn camera master switch ON.

Note

Because the time to wind varies slightly for each camera, exposures will not be made simultaneously during runaway operation. Pictures will, therefore, not be suitable for stereoscopic viewing.

3. Runaway operation may also be obtained by setting the controls for manual operation and holding the trigger down.

AIRPLANE'S AIRSPEED INDICATOR READING—MPH																	INTERVALOMETER SETTING—SEC.																
Airplane's Altimeter Reading (1,000 Ft.) — Altimeter Set at 29.92" Hg.																	Altitude Above Ground — 1,000 Ft.																
6	8	10	12	14	16	18	20	22	24	26	28	30	32	34	36	38	6	8	10	12	14	16	18	20	22	24	26	28	30	32	34	36	38
180	170	165	160	155	150	145	140	130	125								2"	3"	4†	5†	5†	6†	6†	9	9	9	9	12	12	12	15	15	15
210	200	195	185	180	170	165	160	150	145	140	135	125					2"	3"	4†	4†	5†	6†	6†	6†	9	9	9	9	12	12	12	12	12
235	230	220	215	205	195	185	180	170	165	160	150	145	140	135	125		2"	3"	3"	4†	4†	5†	6†	6†	6†	9	9	9	9	9	12	12	12
260	255	245	240	230	225	215	205	195	190	180	170	165	160	150	145	140	2"	2"	3"	3"	4†	5†	5†	6†	6†	6†	9	9	9	9	9	9	12
285	275	270	260	250	245	235	230	220	210	200	190	180	175	170	160	155	2"	2"	3"	3"	4†	4†	5†	5†	6†	6†	6†	6†	9	9	9	9	9
310	300	290	280	275	265	260	250	240	230	220	215	205	195	185	180	170	1"	2"	2"	3"	3"	4†	4†	5†	5†	6†	6†	6†	6†	9	9	9	9
330	320	310	300	295	285	280	270	260	250	240	230	225	215	205	195	190	1"	2"	2"	3"	3"	4†	4†	5†	5†	5†	6†	6†	6†	6†	9	9	9
355	345	335	325	315	310	300	290	280	270	260	250	240	230	225	215	205	1"	2"	2"	3"	3"	3"	4†	4†	5†	5†	5†	6†	6†	6†	6†	9	9
380	370	360	350	340	330	320	310	300	290	280	270	260	250	240	230	220	1"	1"	2"	2"	3"	3"	4†	4†	4†	5†	5†	5†	6†	6†	6†	6†	9

To determine intervalometer setting: (1) Find airplane's altimeter reading in left hand side of table; (2) Follow down to first indicated airspeed higher than airplane's airspeed; (3) Follow across horizontal to intervalometer setting below distance above the ground.

Time intervals marked (") are too short for runaway operation with K-17 camera.

Time intervals marked (†) are too short for runaway operation with K-18 camera.

Figure 34 — Intervalometer Setting (60% Overlap)

APPENDIX I

GLOSSARY OF NOMENCLATURE (U. S. A.–BRITISH)

AMERICAN	BRITISH	AMERICAN	BRITISH
Accumulator (hydraulic)	Pressure reservoir	Lean mixture	Weak mixture
Air filter	Air cleaner	Left	Port
Airfoil	Aerofoil	Level off	Flatten out
Antenna	Aerial	Life raft	Dinghy
Battery (electrical)	Electrical accumulator	Manifold pressure	Boost pressure
Ceiling	Cloud height	Mooring line	Mooring guy
Check valve	Non-return valve	Mooring rings	Picketing rings
Command set (radio)	Pilot controller set	Oil pan	Crankcase sump
Course (direction with respect to true north)	Track angle	Panel (center wing)	Centre section plane
		Panel (outboard)	Outer plane
Critical speed	Stalling speed	Radio mast	Rod aerial
Cylinder (hydraulic)	Jack (hydraulic)	Radio range beacon	Radio track beacon
Drift	Drift-angle	Right	Starboard
Empennage	Tail unit	Screen (oil)	Filter
Flare (signal)	Signal star, signal projectile	Stabilizer (horizontal)	Tail plane
		Stabilizer (vertical)	Fin
Gage (fuel)	Fuel-contents gauge	Tachometer	Engine speed indicator, revolution counter
Gasoline (gas, fuel)	Petrol or fuel		
Generator	Dynamo	Take-off distance	Take-off run
Ground (electrical)	Earth	Tube (radio)	Valve
Gyro horizon	Artificial horizon	Valve (fuel or oil)	Cock
Heading	Course	Weight (empty)	Tare
Indicated air speed (ias)	Air-speed-indicator reading	Weight (gross)	All-up weight
		Windshield	Windscreen
Landing gear	Alighting gear, under-carriage	Wing	Main plane

Flight Operating Charts, Tables, Curves, and Diagrams

1. FLIGHT PLANNING.

The following outline may be used as a guide to assist personnel in the use of the FLIGHT OPERATION IN-STRUCTION CHART for flight planning purposes.

a. If the flight plan calls for a continuous flight where the desired cruising power and air speed are reasonably constant after take-off and climb to 5,000 feet, the fuel required and flight time may be computed as a "single-section flight."

(1) Within the limits of the airplane, the fuel required and flying time for a given mission depend largely upon the speed desired. With all other factors remaining equal in an airplane, speed is obtained at a sacrifice of range, and range is obtained at a sacrifice of speed. The speed is usually determined after considering the urgency of the flight plotted against the range required. The time of take-off is adjusted so as to have the flight arrive at its destination at the predetermined time.

Fuel should be used in the following sequence:

1. Reserve tanks for first 15 minutes.
2. External tanks.
3. Outer wing tanks (if installed).
4. Main tanks.
5. Reserve tanks.

(2) Select the FLIGHT OPERATION INSTRUC-TION CHART corresponding to the weight and external load items of the airplane. Locate the largest figure entered under gph (gallons per hour) in column 1 on the lower half of the chart. Multiply this figure by the number and/or fraction of hours desired for reserve fuel. Add the resulting figure to the number of gallons set forth in footnote No. 2, and subtract the total from the amount of fuel in the airplane prior to starting the engines. The figure obtained as a result of this computation will represent the amount of gasoline available and applicable for flight planning purposes on the "Range in Air Miles" section of the FLIGHT OPERA-TION INSTRUCTION CHART.

(3) Select a figure in the fuel column equal to, or the next entry less than, the available amount of fuel in the airplane as determined in paragraph 2, *a*, (2) above. Move horizontally to the right or left and select a figure equal to, or the next entry greater than the air miles (with no wind) to be flown. Operating values contained in the column number in which this figure appears, represent the highest cruising speed possible at the range desired; however, the airplane may be operated in accordance with values contained under OPER-ATING DATA in any column of a higher number with the flight plan being completed at a sacrifice of speed but at an increase in fuel economy.

(4) Using the same column number selected by application of instructions contained in the preceding paragraph, read the gallons per hour given at the altitude to be flown and divide this figure into the number of gallons available for cruising, as determined in paragraph (2) above. This will give the calculated flight duration in hours, which can then be converted into hours and minutes and deducted from the desired arrival time at destination in order to obtain the take-off time (without consideration for wind). To allow for wind, determine the calculated ground speed by dividing the flight duration in hours into the range selected in paragraph (3) and calculate a new corrected ground speed with the aid of a navigator's triangle of velocities.

(5) The airplane and engine operating values listed below "Operating Data" in any column except I are calculated to give constant miles per gallon at any altitude listed. Therefore, the airplane may be operated at any altitude and at the corresponding set of values given so long as they are in the same column listing the range desired.

Ranges listed in column I under "Max. Cont. Power" are correct only at sea level and 12,000 feet.

(6) The flight plan may be readily changed at any time enroute, and the chart will show the balance of range at various cruising powers by following the "Instructions for Using Chart" printed on each page.

(7) In using the FLIGHT OPERATION IN-STRUCTION CHARTS set the propeller control to give the desired rpm and open the throttle to give the desired indicated air speed. Use the manifold pressure only as an approximate value for reference.

b. If the original flight plan calls for a mission requiring changes in power, speed, or gross load, in accordance with "GR. WT," increments shown in the series of "FLIGHT OPERATION INSTRUCTION CHARTS" provided, the total flight should be broken down into a series of individual short flights, each computed as outlined in paragraph *a,* in its entirety, and then added together to make up the total flight and its requirements.

TAKE-OFF, CLIMB & LANDING CHART

AIRPLANE MODELS P-38H

ENGINE MODELS V-1710-89(RH) / V-1710-91(LH)

SPEC. AN-H-9 / Dec. 18, 1942 / FORM ASC-510

TAKE-OFF DISTANCE (IN FEET)

GROSS WEIGHT (IN LBS.)	HEAD WIND MPH	HEAD WIND KNOTS	HARD SURFACE RUNWAY AT SEA LEVEL GROUND RUN	HARD SURFACE RUNWAY AT SEA LEVEL TO CLEAR 50' OBJ.	AT 3,000 FT. GROUND RUN	AT 3,000 FT. TO CLEAR 50' OBJ.	AT 6,000 FT. GROUND RUN	AT 6,000 FT. TO CLEAR 50' OBJ.	SOD-TURF RUNWAY AT SEA LEVEL GROUND RUN	AT SEA LEVEL TO CLEAR 50' OBJ.	AT 3,000 FT. GROUND RUN	AT 3,000 FT. TO CLEAR 50' OBJ.	AT 6,000 FT. GROUND RUN	AT 6,000 FT. TO CLEAR 50' OBJ.	SOFT SURFACE RUNWAY AT SEA LEVEL GROUND RUN	AT SEA LEVEL TO CLEAR 50' OBJ.	AT 3,000 FT. GROUND RUN	AT 3,000 FT. TO CLEAR 50' OBJ.	AT 6,000 FT. GROUND RUN	AT 6,000 FT. TO CLEAR 50' OBJ.
16,100	0	0	840	1320	950	1510	1100	1770	880	1360	1020	1580	1190	1870	1040	1540	1210	1790	1420	2120
	17	15	600	990	690	1150	790	1350	630	1040	720	1190	850	1410	770	1180	860	1350	1010	1590
	34	30	390	710	450	820	520	970	420	740	470	850	550	1010	480	810	560	950	660	1120
	51	45	220	470	240	530	310	660	240	490	280	570	320	670	280	530	310	610	390	750
18,100	0	0	1140	1790	1300	2080	1510	2511	1180	1840	1380	2180	1620	2630	1450	2140	1720	2550	2010	3070
	17	15	830	1380	960	1620	1110	1960	860	1410	1010	1680	1190	2040	1070	1640	1260	1950	1470	2360
	34	30	560	1010	660	1200	750	1450	590	1040	700	1250	810	1510	730	1190	850	1420	1000	1720
	51	45	340	700	400	830	460	1010	350	710	420	850	500	1050	440	810	510	950	600	1170
19,500	0	0	1370	2220	1580	2660	1840	3340	1470	2330	1710	2800	2000	3510	1840	2750	2150	3280	2560	4130
	17	15	1020	1750	1180	2100	1360	2650	1090	1820	1270	2200	1480	2780	1360	2120	1590	2560	1890	3230
	34	30	710	1310	830	1590	950	2020	760	1370	890	1660	1040	2130	950	1580	1110	1900	1320	2430
	51	45	450	940	530	1140	620	1490	480	970	550	1170	670	1550	600	1100	690	1330	840	1730

NOTE: INCREASE DISTANCE 9 % FOR EACH 10°C ABOVE 0°C (10 % FOR EACH 20°F ABOVE 32°F)

ENGINE LIMITS FOR TAKE-OFF 3000 RPM & 54 IN. HG

CLIMB DATA

COMBAT MISSIONS USE 3000 RPM & 54* IN. HG

FERRY MISSIONS USE 2300 RPM & 35 IN. HG

GROSS WEIGHT IN LBS.	TYPE OF CLIMB	S.L. TO 5,000 FT. ALT. BEST I.A.S. MPH	BEST I.A.S. KNOTS	FT/MIN	TIME FROM S.L.	10,000 BEST I.A.S. MPH	BEST I.A.S. KNOTS	FT/MIN	TIME FROM S.L.	FT. ALT. FUEL FROM S.L. U.S.	IMP.	15,000 BEST I.A.S. MPH	BEST I.A.S. KNOTS	FT/MIN	TIME FROM S.L.	FT. ALT. FUEL FROM S.L. U.S.	IMP.	25,000 BEST I.A.S. MPH	BEST I.A.S. KNOTS	FT/MIN	TIME FROM S.L.	FT. ALT. FUEL FROM S.L. U.S.	IMP.	35,000 BEST I.A.S. MPH	BEST I.A.S. KNOTS	FT/MIN	TIME FROM S.L.	FT. ALT. FUEL FROM S.L. U.S.	IMP.	BLOWER CHANGE
16,100	COMBAT	178	155	3500	2	175	152	3400	3	61	53	172	149	3200	5	69	60	162	141	2500	8	87	75	151	131	1200	13	112	97	
	FERRY	151	131	1700	3	151	131	1600	6	60	52	151	131	1500	9	68	59	151	131	1200	17	87	75	151	131	500	28	116	100	
18,100	COMBAT	178	155	2800	2	175	152	2700	4	65	56	172	149	2500	6	76	66	162	141	1900	10	99	86	151	131	600	18	136	118	
	FERRY	151	131	1200	4	151	131	1200	8	65	56	151	131	1100	13	77	67	151	131	700	24	106	92							
19,500	COMBAT	178	155	2500	2	175	152	2300	4	68	59	172	149	2200	7	80	69	162	141	1600	12	107	93	151	131	400	22	155	134	
	FERRY	151	131	1000	5	151	131	1000	10	70	61	151	131	800	15	84	73	151	131	500	30	122	106							

NOTE: INCREASED ELAPSED CLIMBING TIME 5 % FOR EACH 10°C ABOVE 0°C FREE AIR TEMPERATURE (5 % FOR EACH 20°F ABOVE 32°F) FUEL INCLUDES WARM-UP AND TAKE-OFF ALLOWANCE

LANDING DISTANCE (IN FEET)

GROSS WEIGHT IN LBS.	BEST I.A.S. APPROACH MPH	BEST I.A.S. APPROACH KNOTS	HARD DRY SURFACE AT SEA LEVEL TO CLEAR 50' OBJ.	AT SEA LEVEL GROUND ROLL	AT 3,000 FT. TO CLEAR 50' OBJ.	AT 3,000 FT. GROUND ROLL	AT 6,000 FT. TO CLEAR 50' OBJ.	AT 6,000 FT. GROUND ROLL	FIRM DRY SOD AT SEA LEVEL TO CLEAR 50' OBJ.	AT SEA LEVEL GROUND ROLL	AT 3,000 FT. TO CLEAR 50' OBJ.	AT 3,000 FT. GROUND ROLL	AT 6,000 FT. TO CLEAR 50' OBJ.	AT 6,000 FT. GROUND ROLL	WET OR SLIPPERY AT SEA LEVEL TO CLEAR 50' OBJ.	AT SEA LEVEL GROUND ROLL	AT 3,000 FT. TO CLEAR 50' OBJ.	AT 3,000 FT. GROUND ROLL	AT 6,000 FT. TO CLEAR 50' OBJ.	AT 6,000 FT. GROUND ROLL
13,500	115	101	1760	1170	1920	1300	2100	1460	1920	1330	2100	1480	2310	1660	4070	3480	4500	3880	5000	4350
15,500	120	104	1950	1330	2130	1480	2350	1660	2140	1520	2350	1700	2590	1900	4590	3970	5080	4430	5650	4960

NOTE: FOR GROUND TEMPERATURES ABOVE 35°C (95°F) INCREASE APPROACH I.A.S. 10% AND ALLOW 20% INCREASE IN GROUND ROLL.

REMARKS * FOR COMBAT CLIMB USE 3000 R.P.M. AND 54 IN. HG. TO 20,000 FEET. REDUCE MAN. PRESS. AS FOLLOWS ABOVE 20,000 FT. STILL USING 3000 R.P.M.

	ALTITUDE 25,000	30,000	35,000	40,000
TYPE B-13 TURBOS	45	35	30	20
TYPE B-33 TURBOS	52	49	41	33

LEGEND:
I.A.S.: Indicated Air Speed
M.P.H.: Miles Per Hour
S.L.: Sea Level
U.S.: U. S. Gallons
IMP.: Imperial Gallons
NOTE: All Distances are Average

RED FIGURES HAVE NOT BEEN FLIGHT CHECKED

SPEC. AN-H-8 Dec. 18, 1942 FORM ASC-510

AIRPLANE MODELS

P-38J

F-5B

TAKE-OFF, CLIMB & LANDING CHART

TAKE-OFF DISTANCE (IN FEET)

ENGINE MODELS

V-1710-89(RH)

V-1710-91(LH)

GROSS WEIGHT (IN LBS.)	HEAD WIND		HARD SURFACE RUNWAY						SOD-TURF RUNWAY						SOFT SURFACE RUNWAY					
			AT SEA LEVEL		AT 3,000 FT.		AT 6,000 FT.		AT SEA LEVEL		AT 3,000 FT.		AT 6,000 FT.		AT SEA LEVEL		AT 3,000 FT.		AT 6,000 FT.	
	MPH	KNOTS	GROUND RUN	TO CLEAR 50' OBJ.	GROUND RUN	TO CLEAR 50' OBJ.	GROUND RUN	TO CLEAR 50' OBJ.	GROUND RUN	TO CLEAR 50' OBJ.	GROUND RUN	TO CLEAR 50' OBJ.	GROUND RUN	TO CLEAR 50' OBJ.	GROUND RUN	TO CLEAR 50' OBJ.	GROUND RUN	TO CLEAR 50' OBJ.	GROUND RUN	TO CLEAR 50' OBJ.
17,400	0	0	1030	1620	1170	1850	1360	2210	1060	1650	1240	1940	1450	2330	1290	1900	1530	2250	1780	2680
	17	15	750	1230	860	1440	990	1720	770	1260	900	1490	1060	1780	950	1460	1110	1710	1300	2040
	34	30	500	890	580	1050	660	1260	520	910	620	1080	710	1300	630	1050	740	1230	870	1490
	51	45	300	610	340	700	390	850	310	620	370	730	430	890	380	680	430	810	520	990
19,400	0	0	1350	2190	1560	2620	1810	3280	1450	2300	1680	2750	1970	3440	1810	2710	2120	3230	2510	4040
	17	15	1000	1720	1160	2060	1350	2600	1070	1800	1250	2160	1470	2730	1340	2090	1570	2520	1870	3160
	34	30	690	1290	820	1560	940	1970	750	1350	880	1630	1030	2070	930	1550	1090	1870	1310	2390
	51	45	440	920	520	1120	610	1450	470	950	540	1140	660	1510	590	1070	680	1310	820	1690
21,400	0	0	1740	2910	2000	3560	2320	4960	1860	3040	2180	3760	2560	5220	2490	3730	2920	4570	3500	6260
	17	15	1300	2400	1520	2840	1760	4020	1390	2500	1650	2990	1930	4200	1870	3030	2200	3590	2640	4990
	34	30	930	1740	1090	2180	1260	3140	990	1810	1190	2290	1390	3280	1330	2190	1560	2700	1900	3840
	51	45	610	1250	730	1610	830	2330	660	1310	790	1660	920	2430	860	1530	1030	1930	1250	2800

NOTE: INCREASE DISTANCE 9 % FOR EACH 10°C ABOVE 0°C (10 % FOR EACH 20°F ABOVE 32°F)   ENGINE LIMITS FOR TAKE-OFF 3000 RPM & 54 IN. HG

CLIMB DATA

COMBAT MISSIONS USE 3000 RPM & 54 IN. HG *

FERRY MISSIONS USE 2300 RPM & 35 IN. HG

GROSS WEIGHT IN LBS.	TYPE OF CLIMB	S.L. TO 5000 FT. ALT.				10,000 FT. ALT.				15,000 FT. ALT.					25,000 FT. ALT.				35,000 FT. ALT.					BLOWER CHANGE
		BEST I.A.S.		FT/MIN	TIME FROM S.L.	BEST I.A.S.		FT/MIN	TIME FROM S.L.	BEST I.A.S.		FT/MIN	FUEL FROM S.L.		BEST I.A.S.		FT/MIN	TIME FROM S.L.	FUEL FROM S.L.		BEST I.A.S.		FT/MIN	TIME FROM S.L.	FUEL FROM S.L.	
		MPH	KNOTS			MPH	KNOTS			MPH	KNOTS		U.S.	IMP.	MPH	KNOTS			U.S.	IMP.	MPH	KNOTS			U.S.	IMP.	
17,400	COMBAT	180	156	3200	2	178	154	3100	4	59	49	175	152	2900	5	69	57	170	148	2400	9	89	74	165	143	1000	15	112	93	
	FERRY	160	139	1400	4	160	139	1400	7	57	48	160	139	1400	11	66	55	160	139	1100	19	85	71	160	139	500	33	117	97	
19,400	COMBAT	180	156	2600	2	178	154	2400	4	63	53	175	152	2300	7	75	62	170	148	1800	11	103	86	165	143	500	20	139	116	
	FERRY	160	139	1100	5	160	139	1100	10	62	52	160	139	1000	15	72	60	160	139	700	27	101	84	—	—	—	—	—	—	
21,400	COMBAT	185	161	2200	3	183	159	2000	5	67	56	180	156	1900	8	81	67	175	152	1400	14	116	97	170	148	200	27	168	140	
	FERRY	165	143	800	7	165	143	700	13	71	59	165	143	700	20	87	72	165	143	300	40	135	112	—	—	—	—	—	—	

NOTE: INCREASED ELAPSED CLIMBING TIME 5 % FOR EACH 10°C ABOVE 0°C FREE AIR TEMPERATURE (5 % FOR EACH 20°F ABOVE 32°F)   FUEL INCLUDES WARM-UP AND TAKE-OFF ALLOWANCE

LANDING DISTANCE (IN FEET)

GROSS WEIGHT IN LBS.	BEST I.A.S. APPROACH		HARD DRY SURFACE						FIRM DRY SOD						WET OR SLIPPERY					
			AT SEA LEVEL		AT 3,000 FT.		AT 6,000 FT.		AT SEA LEVEL		AT 3,000 FT.		AT 6,000 FT.		AT SEA LEVEL		AT 3,000 FT.		AT 6,000 FT.	
	MPH	KNOTS	TO CLEAR 50' OBJ.	GROUND ROLL	TO CLEAR 50' OBJ.	GROUND ROLL	TO CLEAR 50' OBJ.	GROUND ROLL	TO CLEAR 50' OBJ.	GROUND ROLL	TO CLEAR 50' OBJ.	GROUND ROLL	TO CLEAR 50' OBJ.	GROUND ROLL	TO CLEAR 50' OBJ.	GROUND ROLL	TO CLEAR 50' OBJ.	GROUND ROLL	TO CLEAR 50' OBJ.	GROUND ROLL
14,000	120	104	1800	1090	1960	1220	2160	1370	1970	1250	2160	1400	2370	1560	4190	3270	4630	3650	5150	4080
16,000	125	109	2010	1260	2200	1400	2430	1570	2210	1440	2420	1600	2670	1790	4750	3750	5260	4180	5850	4690

NOTE: FOR GROUND TEMPERATURES ABOVE 35°C (95°F) INCREASE APPROACH I.A.S. 10% AND ALLOW 20% INCREASE IN GROUND ROLL.

REMARKS * FOR COMBAT CLIMB USE 3000 R.P.M. AND 54 IN. HG. TO 26,600 FEET THEN GRADUALLY REDUCE MANIFOLD PRESSURE TO 48.5 IN. HG. AT 30,000 FEET AND TO 41.0 IN. HG. AT 35,000 FT.

LEGEND
I.A.S.: Indicated Air Speed
M.P.H.: Miles Per Hour
S.L.: Sea Level
U.S.: U. S. Gallons
IMP.: Imperial Gallons
NOTE: All Distances are Average
RED FIGURES HAVE NOT BEEN FLIGHT CHECKED

SPEC. AN-H-8
Dec. 18, 1942
FORM ASC-510

TAKE-OFF, CLIMB & LANDING CHART

AIRPLANE MODELS

P-38L

ENGINE MODELS

V-1710-111(R'H)

V-1710-113(LH)

TAKE-OFF DISTANCE (IN FEET)

GROSS WEIGHT (IN LBS.)	HEAD WIND		HARD SURFACE RUN-WAY						SOD-TURF RUNWAY						SOFT SURFACE RUNWAY					
			AT SEA LEVEL		AT 3,000 FT.		AT 6,000 FT.		AT SEA LEVEL		AT 3,000 FT.		AT 6,000 FT.		AT SEA LEVEL		AT 3,000 FT.		AT 6,000 FT.	
	MPH	KNOTS	GROUND RUN	TO CLEAR 50' OBJ.	GROUND RUN	TO CLEAR 50' OBJ.	GROUND RUN	TO CLEAR 50' OBJ.	GROUND RUN	TO CLEAR 50' OBJ.	GROUND RUN	TO CLEAR 50' OBJ.	GROUND RUN	TO CLEAR 50' OBJ.	GROUND RUN	TO CLEAR 50' OBJ.	GROUND RUN	TO CLEAR 50' OBJ.	GROUND RUN	TO CLEAR 50' OBJ.
17,400	0	0	1030	1620	1170	1850	1360	2210	1060	1650	1240	1940	1450	2330	1290	1900	1530	2250	1780	2680
	17	15	750	1230	860	1440	990	1720	770	1260	900	1490	1060	1780	950	1460	1110	1710	1300	2040
	34	30	500	890	580	1050	660	1260	520	910	620	1080	710	1300	630	1050	740	1230	870	1490
	51	45	300	610	340	700	390	850	310	620	370	730	430	890	380	680	430	810	520	990
19,400	0	0	1350	2190	1560	2620	1810	3280	1450	2300	1680	2750	1970	3440	1810	2710	2120	3230	2510	4040
	17	15	1000	1720	1160	2060	1350	2600	1070	1800	1250	2160	1470	2730	1340	2090	1570	2520	1870	3160
	34	30	690	1290	820	1560	940	1970	750	1350	880	1630	1030	2070	930	1550	1090	1870	1310	2390
	51	45	440	920	520	1120	610	1450	470	950	540	1140	660	1510	590	1070	680	1310	820	1690
21,400	0	0	1740	2910	2000	3560	2320	4960	1860	3040	2180	3760	2560	5220	2490	3730	2920	4570	3500	6260
	17	15	1300	2400	1520	2840	1760	4020	1390	2500	1650	2990	1930	4200	1870	3030	2200	3590	2640	4990
	34	30	930	1740	1090	2180	1260	3140	990	1810	1190	2290	1390	3280	1330	2190	1560	2700	1900	3840
	51	45	610	1250	730	1610	830	2330	660	1310	790	1660	920	2430	860	1530	1030	1930	1250	2800

NOTE: INCREASE DISTANCE 9 % FOR EACH 10°C ABOVE 0°C (10 % FOR EACH 20°F ABOVE 32°F)   ENGINE LIMITS FOR TAKE-OFF 3000 RPM & 54 IN. HG

CLIMB DATA

COMBAT MISSIONS USE 3000 RPM & 54 IN. HG *   FERRY MISSIONS USE 2300 RPM & 35 IN. HG

GROSS WEIGHT IN LBS.	TYPE O. CLIMB	S. L. TO 5000 FT. ALT.				10,000			FT. ALT.			15,000			FT. ALT.			25,000			FT. ALT.			35,000			FT. ALT.			BLOWER CHANGE
		BEST I.A.S.		FT/MIN	TIME FROM S.L.	BEST I.A.S.		FT/MIN	TIME FROM S.L.	FUEL FROM S.L.		BEST I.A.S.		FT/MIN	TIME FROM S.L.	FUEL FROM S.L.		BEST I.A.S.		FT/MIN	TIME FROM S.L.	FUEL FROM S.L.		BEST I.A.S.		FT/MIN	TIME FROM S.L.	FUEL FROM S.L.		
		MPH	KNOTS			MPH	KNOTS			U.S.	IMP.	MPH	KNOTS			U.S.	IMP.	MPH	KNOTS			U.S.	IMP.	MPH	KNOTS			U.S.	IMP.	
17,400	COMBAT	180	156	3200	2	178	154	3100	4	59	49	175	152	2900	5	69	57	170	148	2400	9	89	74	165	143	1000	15	112	93	
	FERRY	160	139	1400	4	160	139	1400	7	57	48	160	139	1400	11	66	55	160	139	1100	19	85	71	160	139	500	33	117	97	
19,400	COMBAT	180	156	2600	2	178	154	2400	4	63	53	175	152	2300	7	75	62	170	148	1800	11	103	86	165	143	500	20	139	116	
	FERRY	160	139	1100	5	160	139	1100	10	62	52	160	139	1000	15	72	60	160	139	700	27	101	84							
21,400	COMBAT	185	161	2200	3	183	159	2000	5	67	56	180	156	1900	8	81	67	175	152	1400	14	116	97	170	148	200	27	168	140	
	FERRY	165	143	800	7	165	143	700	13	71	59	165	143	700	20	87	72	165	143	300	40	135	112							

NOTE: INCREASED ELAPSED CLIMBING TIME 5 % FOR EACH 10°C ABOVE 0°C FREE AIR TEMPERATURE (5 % FOR EACH 20°F ABOVE 32°F)   FUEL INCLUDES WARM-UP AND TAKE-OFF ALLOWANCE

LANDING DISTANCE (IN FEET)

GROSS WEIGHT IN LBS.	BEST I.A.S. APPROACH		HARD DRY SURFACE						FIRM DRY SOD						WET OR SLIPPERY					
			AT SEA LEVEL		AT 3,000 FT.		AT 6,000 FT.		AT SEA LEVEL		AT 3,000 FT.		AT 6,000 FT.		AT SEA LEVEL		AT 3,000 FT.		AT 6,000 FT.	
	MPH	KNOTS	TO CLEAR 50' OBJ.	GROUND ROLL	TO CLEAR 50' OBJ.	GROUND ROLL	TO CLEAR 50' OBJ.	GROUND ROLL	TO CLEAR 50' OBJ.	GROUND ROLL	TO CLEAR 50' OBJ.	GROUND ROLL	TO CLEAR 50' OBJ.	GROUND ROLL	TO CLEAR 50' OBJ.	GROUND ROLL	TO CLEAR 50' OBJ.	GROUND ROLL	TO CLEAR 50' OBJ.	GROUND ROLL
14,000	120	104	1800	1090	1960	1220	2160	1370	1970	1250	2160	1400	2370	1560	4190	3270	4630	3650	5150	4080
16,000	125	109	2010	1260	2200	1400	2430	1570	2210	1440	2420	1600	2670	1790	4750	3750	5260	4180	5850	4690

NOTE: FOR GROUND TEMPERATURES ABOVE 35°C (95°F) INCREASE APPROACH I.A.S. 10% AND ALLOW 20% INCREASE IN GROUND ROLL.

REMARKS * FOR COMBAT CLIMB USE 3000 R.P.M. AND 54 IN. HG. TO 26,600 FEET THEN GRADUALLY REDUCE MANIFOLD PRESSURE TO 48.5 IN. HG. AT 30,000 FEET AND TO 41.0 IN. HG. AT 35,000 FEET.

LEGEND
I.A.S.: Indicated Air Speed
M.P.H.: Miles Per Hour
S.L.: Sea Level
U.S.: U. S. Gallons
IMP.: Imperial Gallons
NOTE: All Distances are Average
RED FIGURES HAVE NOT BEEN FLIGHT CHECKED

MODEL(S)	FLIGHT OPERATION INSTRUCTION CHART	EXTERNAL LOAD ITEMS
P-38H		TANK SUPPORTS ONLY
ENGINE(S): V-1710-89 & V-1710-91	CHART WEIGHT LIMITS: 16,100 TO 13,500 POUNDS	

LIMITS	R.P.M.	M.P. (IN. HG.)	BLOWER POSITION	MIXTURE POSITION	TIME LIMIT	TOTAL G.P.H.
WAR MAX.	3000	60		AR	5	360
MILITARY POWER	3000	54		AR	15	334
NORMAL RATED	2600	44		AR	NONE	226

INSTRUCTIONS FOR USING CHART: Select figure in FUEL column equal to or less than amount of fuel to be used for cruising. Move horizontally to left or right and select RANGE value equal to or greater than the statute or nautical air miles to be flown. Vertically below and opposite desired cruising altitude (ALT.) read optimum R. P. M., I. A. S. and MIXTURE setting required.

NOTES: Column I is for emergency high speed cruising only. Columns II, III, IV and V give progressive increase in range at a sacrifice in speed. Manifold pressure (M. P.), gallons per hour (G. P. H.) and true airspeed (T. A. S.) are approximate values for reference. For efficiency maintain indicated airspeed (I. A. S.) hourly. Adjust RPM slightly if necessary to avoid exceeding manifold pressure more than 3 in. Hg.

I — STATUTE AT S.L.	I — STATUTE AT 12,000	I — NAUTICAL AT S.L.	I — NAUTICAL AT 12,000	FUEL U.S. GAL.	II — STATUTE	II — NAUTICAL	III — STATUTE	III — NAUTICAL	IV — STATUTE	IV — NAUTICAL	FUEL U.S. GAL.	V — STATUTE	V — NAUTICAL
				300	○ 50 GAL. ALLOWANCE NOT AVAILABLE IN FLIGHT ○						300	960	830
280	320	240	270	250	430	380	610	530	780	680	250	950	830
260	290	220	250	230	400	350	560	490	720	620	230	870	760
230	260	200	230	210	360	320	510	450	650	570	210	800	690
210	240	180	210	190	330	290	470	400	590	510	190	720	630
190	210	160	190	170	290	260	420	360	530	460	170	650	560
170	190	140	160	150	260	230	370	320	470	410	150	570	500
140	160	120	140	130	220	200	320	280	400	350	130	490	430
120	140	110	120	110	190	170	270	230	340	300	110	420	360
100	110	90	100	90	160	140	220	190	280	240	90	340	300
80	90	70	80	70	120	110	170	150	220	190	70	270	230
60	60	50	50	50	90	80	120	110	160	140	50	190	170

MAXIMUM CONTINUOUS — R.P.M.	I.A.S. M.P.H.	MIX-TURE	M.P. In. Hg.	G.P.H.	T.A.S.	ALT. Feet	OPERATING DATA — R.P.M.	I.A.S. M.P.H.	MIX-TURE	M.P. In. Hg.	G.P.H.	T.A.S.	OPERATING DATA — R.P.M.	I.A.S. M.P.H.	MIX-TURE	M.P. In. Hg.	G.P.H.	T.A.S.	OPERATING DATA — R.P.M.	I.A.S. M.P.H.	MIX-TURE	M.P. In. Hg.	G.P.H.	T.A.S.	ALT. Feet	MAXIMUM RANGE — R.P.M.	I.A.S. M.P.H.	MIX-TURE	M.P. In. Hg.	G.P.H.	T.A.S.
2600	238	A.R.	44	245	396	30000	2450	245	A.R.	39	197	378	2300	228	A.L.	35	130	355	2000	199	A.L.	30	93	321	30000						
2600	272	A.R.	44	245	384	25000	2450	258	A.R.	38	191	367	2250	241	A.L.	34	126	343	1900	213	A.L.	30	90	310	25000	1700	181	A.L.	26	64	272
2600	285	A.R.	44	245	370	20000	2400	267	A.R.	38	182	349	2150	250	A.L.	34	120	326	1750	222	A.L.	31	85	293	20000	1600	184	A.L.	26	59	254
2600	293	A.R.	44	245	353	15000	2400	273	A.R.	37	172	330	2050	253	A.L.	34	113	307	1600	224	A.L.	31	79	274	15000	1600	183	A.L.	24	55	234
2600	299	A.R.	44	245	343	12000	2350	275	A.R.	36	164	316	2000	253	A.L.	33	108	292	1600	223	A.L.	30	75	261	12000	1600	180	A.L.	24	52	220
2600	303	A.R.	44	245	332	9000	2350	276	A.R.	36	158	304	1900	253	A.L.	33	103	280	1600	222	A.L.	29	72	248	9000	1600	176	A.L.	23	50	208
2600	307	A.R.	44	245	322	6000	2350	276	A.R.	35	152	291	1850	254	A.L.	33	99	270	1600	221	A.L.	28	68	236	6000	1600	175	A.L.	22	47	196
2600	311	A.R.	44	245	311	3000	2300	280	A.R.	35	147	282	1800	255	A.L.	33	94	257	1600	219	A.L.	27	65	224	3000	1600	173	A.L.	21	44	185
2600	314	A.R.	44	245	302	S.L.	2300	283	A.R.	34	142	273	1700	254	A.L.	33	91	247	1600	217	A.L.	26	62	213	S.L.	1600	173	A.L.	21	42	177

NOTES

○ ALLOW 50 GAL. FOR WARM-UP, TAKE-OFF & INITIAL CLIMB PLUS ALLOWANCE FOR WIND, RESERVE & COMBAT AS REQ'D.

EXAMPLE

AT 15,800 LB. GROSS WT. WITH 250 GAL. OF FUEL (AFTER DEDUCTING TOTAL ALLOWANCES OF 50 GAL.) TO FLY 780 STAT. AIRMILES AT 12,000 FT. ALT. MAINTAIN 1600 RPM AND 223 MPH IND. AIRSPEED WITH MIXTURE SET A.L.

LEGEND

I. A. S.: INDICATED AIRSPEED
M. P.: MANIFOLD PRESSURE
G. P. H.: U. S. GAL. PER HOUR
T. A. S.: TRUE AIRSPEED
S. L.: SEA LEVEL

F. T.: FULL THROTTLE
F. R.: FULL RICH
A. R.: AUTO-RICH
A. L.: AUTO-LEAN
C. L.: CRUISING LEAN

RED FIGURES ARE PRELIMINARY, SUBJECT TO REVISION AFTER FLIGHT CHECK

FLIGHT OPERATION INSTRUCTION CHART

MODEL(S): P-38H

EXTERNAL LOAD ITEMS: TWO 165 GALLON TANKS

ENGINE(S): V-1710-89 & V-1710-91

CHART WEIGHT LIMITS: 18,100 TO 13,500 POUNDS

LIMITS	R.P.M.	M.P. (IN. HG.)	BLOWER POSITION	MIXTURE POSITION	TIME LIMIT	TOTAL G.P.H.
WAR MAX.	3000	60		AR	5	360
MILITARY POWER	3000	54		AR	15	334
NORMAL RATED	2600	44		AR	NONE	226

INSTRUCTIONS FOR USING CHART: Select figure in FUEL column equal to or less than amount of fuel to be used for cruising. Move horizontally to left or right and select RANGE value equal to or greater than the statute or nautical air miles to be flown. Vertically below and opposite desired cruising altitude (ALT.) read optimum R. P. M., I. A. S. and MIXTURE setting required.

NOTES: Column I is for emergency high speed cruising only. Columns II, III, IV and V give progressive increase in range at a sacrifice in speed. Manifold pressure (M. P.), gallons per hour (G. P. H.) and true airspeed (T. A. S.) are approximate values for reference. For efficiency maintain indicated airspeed (I. A. S.) hourly. Adjust RPM slightly if necessary to avoid exceeding manifold pressure more than 3 in. Hg.

I RANGE IN AIR MILES				FUEL U.S. GAL.	II RANGE IN AIR MILES		III RANGE IN AIR MILES		IV RANGE IN AIR MILES		FUEL U.S. GAL.	V RANGE IN AIR MILES	
STATUTE		NAUTICAL			STATUTE	NAUTICAL	STATUTE	NAUTICAL	STATUTE	NAUTICAL		STATUTE	NAUTICAL
AT S.L.	AT 12,000	AT S.L.	AT 12,000	630	○ 60 GAL. ALLOWANCE NOT AVAILABLE IN FLIGHT ○						630	1640	1420
580	660	500	570	570	850	740	1110	960	1370	1190	570	1630	1420
530	600	460	520	520	770	670	1010	880	1250	1090	520	1490	1290
480	540	420	470	470	700	610	910	790	1130	980	470	1340	1170
430	480	370	420	420	630	540	810	710	1010	880	420	1200	1050
380	430	330	370	370	550	480	720	630	890	770	370	1060	920
330	370	280	320	320	480	410	620	540	770	670	320	920	800
280	310	240	270	270	400	350	520	460	650	560	270	770	670
220	250	190	220	220	330	280	430	370	530	460	220	630	550
170	200	150	170	170	250	220	330	290	410	360	170	490	420
120	140	110	120	120	180	150	230	200	290	250	120	340	300
70	80	60	70	70	100	90	140	120	170	150	70	200	170

MAXIMUM CONTINUOUS / **OPERATING DATA** / **MAXIMUM RANGE**

R.P.M.	I.A.S. M.P.H.	MIX-TURE	M.P. In. Hg.	G.P.H.	T.A.S.	ALT. Feet	R.P.M.	I.A.S. M.P.H.	MIX-TURE	M.P. In. Hg.	G.P.H.	T.A.S.	R.P.M.	I.A.S. M.P.H.	MIX-TURE	M.P. In. Hg.	G.P.H.	T.A.S.	R.P.M.	I.A.S. M.P.H.	MIX-TURE	M.P. In. Hg.	G.P.H.	T.A.S.	ALT. Feet	R.P.M.	I.A.S. M.P.H.	MIX-TURE	M.P. In. Hg.	G.P.H.	T.A.S.
2600	232	A.R.	44	245	360	30000	2500	222	A.R.	40	211	347	2300	200	A.R.	35	149	322	2150	187	A.L.	33	114	306	30000						
2600	248	A.R.	44	245	353	25000	2500	238	A.R.	40	205	339	2300	218	A.R.	35	146	315	2050	202	A.L.	33	111	298	25000	1850	178	A.L.	30	85	269
2600	259	A.R.	44	245	339	20000	2450	245	A.R.	39	195	322	2300	228	A.L.	35	130	300	1950	211	A.L.	33	105	282	20000	1700	182	A.L.	30	79	252
2600	268	A.R.	44	245	324	15000	2450	251	A.R.	38	185	305	2300	237	A.L.	35	130	288	1850	217	A.L.	33	100	267	15000	1600	185	A.L.	30	74	236
2600	273	A.R.	44	245	314	12000	2400	253	A.R.	37	178	292	2300	240	A.L.	35	130	278	1800	217	A.L.	33	95	255	12000	1600	184	A.L.	29	70	224
2600	276	A.R.	44	245	304	9000	2400	255	A.R.	37	171	282	2200	242	A.L.	34	125	268	1750	218	A.L.	33	91	244	9000	1600	183	A.L.	28	67	212
2600	279	A.R.	44	245	295	6000	2350	257	A.R.	36	163	271	2150	243	A.L.	34	120	257	1650	218	A.L.	33	87	233	6000	1600	180	A.L.	27	63	200
2600	285	A.R.	44	245	286	3000	2350	259	A.R.	36	158	262	2100	244	A.L.	34	115	247	1600	218	A.L.	32	83	223	3000	1600	177	A.L.	26	59	189
2600	288	A.R.	44	245	278	S.L.	2350	261	A.R.	35	154	253	2000	244	A.L.	34	110	237	1600	217	A.L.	32	80	213	S.L.	1600	175	A.L.	25	56	179

NOTES

○ ALLOW 60 GAL. FOR WARM-UP, TAKE-OFF & INITIAL CLIMB PLUS ALLOWANCE FOR WIND, RESERVE & COMBAT AS REQ'D.

EXAMPLE

AT 17,740 LB. GROSS WT. WITH 570 GAL. OF FUEL (AFTER DEDUCTING TOTAL ALLOWANCES OF 60 GAL.) TO FLY 1370 STAT. AIRMILES AT 12,000 FT. ALT. MAINTAIN 1800 RPM AND 217 MPH IND. AIRSPEED WITH MIXTURE SET A.L.

LEGEND

- I. A. S.: INDICATED AIRSPEED
- M. P.: MANIFOLD PRESSURE
- G. P. H.: U. S. GAL. PER HOUR
- T. A. S.: TRUE AIRSPEED
- S. L.: SEA LEVEL
- F. T.: FULL THROTTLE
- F. R.: FULL RICH
- A. R.: AUTO-RICH
- A. L.: AUTO-LEAN
- C. L.: CRUISING LEAN

MODEL(S)	FLIGHT OPERATION INSTRUCTION CHART	EXTERNAL LOAD ITEMS
P-38H		TWO 300 GALLON TANKS
ENGINE(S): V-1710-89 & V-1710-91	CHART WEIGHT LIMITS: 19,500 TO 13,700 POUNDS	

LIMITS	R. P. M.	M. P. (IN. HG.)	BLOWER POSITION	MIXTURE POSITION	TIME LIMIT	TOTAL G. P. H.
WAR MAX.	3000	60		AR	5	360
MILITARY POWER	3000	54		AR	15	334
NORMAL RATED	2600	44		AR	NONE	226

INSTRUCTIONS FOR USING CHART: Select figure in FUEL column equal to or less than amount of fuel to be used for cruising. Move horizontally to left or right and select RANGE value equal to or greater than the statute or nautical air miles to be flown. Vertically below and opposite desired cruising altitude (ALT.) read optimum R. P. M., I. A. S. and MIXTURE setting required.

NOTES: Column I is for emergency high speed cruising only. Columns II, III, IV and V give progressive increase in range at a sacrifice in speed. Manifold pressure (M. P.), gallons per hour (G. P. H.) and true airspeed (T. A. S.) are approximate values for reference. For efficiency maintain indicated airspeed (I. A. S.) hourly. Adjust RPM slightly if necessary to avoid exceeding manifold pressure more than 3 in. Hg.

I RANGE IN AIR MILES		FUEL U.S. GAL.	II RANGE IN AIR MILES		III RANGE IN AIR MILES		IV RANGE IN AIR MILES		FUEL U.S. GAL.	V RANGE IN AIR MILES	
STATUTE	NAUTICAL		STATUTE	NAUTICAL	STATUTE	NAUTICAL	STATUTE	NAUTICAL		STATUTE	NAUTICAL
		900	○ 60 GAL. ALLOWANCE NOT AVAILABLE IN FLIGHT ○						900	2210	1920
		840	1180	1030	1510	1310	1840	1600	840	2200	1910
		810	1130	990	1460	1260	1780	1550	810	2110	1840
		730	1020	890	1310	1140	1610	1390	730	1910	1660
		650	910	790	1170	1010	1430	1240	650	1700	1480
Use Column 2		570	800	700	1030	890	1250	1090	570	1490	1290
		490	690	600	880	760	1080	940	490	1280	1110
		410	570	500	740	640	900	780	410	1070	930
		330	460	400	590	510	730	630	330	860	750
		250	350	310	450	390	550	480	250	650	570
		170	240	210	310	270	370	320	170	440	390
		90	130	110	160	140	200	170	90	230	200

MAXIMUM CONTINUOUS						ALT. Feet	OPERATING DATA (II)						OPERATING DATA (III)						OPERATING DATA (IV)						ALT. Feet	MAXIMUM RANGE (V)					
R.P.M.	I.A.S. M.P.H.	MIX-TURE	M.P. In. Hg.	G.P.H.	T.A.S.		R.P.M.	I.A.S. M.P.H.	MIX-TURE	M.P. In. Hg.	G.P.H.	T.A.S.	R.P.M.	I.A.S. M.P.H.	MIX-TURE	M.P. In. Hg.	G.P.H.	T.A.S.	R.P.M.	I.A.S. M.P.H.	MIX-TURE	M.P. In. Hg.	G.P.H.	T.A.S.		R.P.M.	I.A.S. M.P.H.	MIX-TURE	M.P. In. Hg.	G.P.H.	T.A.S.
Use Column 2						30000	2550	216	A.R.	41	219	340	2350	195	A.R.	36	157	316	2200	185	A.L.	34	123	303	30000						
						25000	2500	233	A.R.	40	213	332	2350	211	A.R.	35	153	307	2200	200	A.L.	34	121	296	25000						
						20000	2500	241	A.R.	39	203	316	2300	223	A.R.	35	147	295	2100	209	A.L.	34	115	281	20000	1750	182	A.L.	31	87	252
						15000	2450	242	A.R.	38	192	300	2300	230	A.R.	34	141	281	2000	216	A.L.	33	109	266	15000	1600	188	A.L.	32	82	238
Max. Permissible IAS with 300 gallon tanks-250 MPH.						12000	2400	249	A.R.	38	184	288	2300	234	A.L.	35	130	272	1950	217	A.L.	33	104	254	12000	1600	186	A.L.	31	78	226
						9000	2400	250	A.R.	37	178	277	2300	239	A.L.	35	130	265	1900	218	A.L.	33	100	246	9000	1600	184	A.L.	30	73	214
Use Column 3						6000	Use Column 3 — Max. Permissible IAS with 300 gallon tanks-250 MPH.						2250	241	A.L.	34	127	255	1800	219	A.L.	33	96	234	6000	1600	182	A.L.	29	69	202
						3000							2200	242	A.L.	34	122	245	1750	220	A.L.	33	92	224	3000	1600	180	A.L.	28	66	191
						S.L.							2100	243	A.L.	34	118	236	1700	220	A.L.	32	88	215	S.L.	1600	177	A.L.	27	62	181

NOTES

○ ALLOW 60 GAL. FOR WARM-UP, TAKE-OFF & INITIAL CLIMB PLUS ALLOWANCE FOR WIND, RESERVE & COMBAT AS REQ'D.

EXAMPLE

AT 19,500 LB. GROSS WT. WITH 900 GAL. OF FUEL (AFTER DEDUCTING TOTAL ALLOWANCES OF 60 GAL.) TO FLY 1800 STAT. AIRMILES AT 12,000 FT. ALT. MAINTAIN 1950 RPM AND 217 MPH IND. AIRSPEED WITH MIXTURE SET A.L.

LEGEND

I. A. S.: INDICATED AIRSPEED
M. P.: MANIFOLD PRESSURE
G. P. H.: U. S. GAL. PER HOUR
T. A. S.: TRUE AIRSPEED
S. L.: SEA LEVEL

F. T.: FULL THROTTLE
F. R.: FULL RICH
A. R.: AUTO-RICH
A. L.: AUTO-LEAN
C. L.: CRUISING LEAN

<table>
<tr><td colspan="6">MODEL(S)
P-38H
SINGLE ENGINE OPERATION
ENGINE(S): V-1710-89 & V-1710-91</td><td colspan="6">FLIGHT OPERATION INSTRUCTION CHART
CHART WEIGHT LIMITS: 15,700 TO 13,500 POUNDS</td><td colspan="6">EXTERNAL LOAD ITEMS
SINGLE ENGINE OPERATION
DEAD PROPELLER FEATHERED
EXTERNAL TANK SUPPORTS ONLY</td></tr>
</table>

LIMITS	R.P.M.	M.P. (IN. HG.)	BLOWER POSITION	MIXTURE POSITION	TIME LIMIT	TOTAL G.P.H.
WAR MAX.	3000	60		AR	5	360
MILITARY POWER	3000	54		AR	15	334
NORMAL RATED	2600	44		AR	NONE	226

INSTRUCTIONS FOR USING CHART: Select figure in FUEL column equal to or less than amount of fuel to be used for cruising. Move horizontally to left or right and select RANGE value equal to or greater than the statute or nautical air miles to be flown. Vertically below and opposite desired cruising altitude (ALT.) read optimum R. P. M., I. A. S. and MIXTURE setting required.

NOTES: Column I is for emergency high speed cruising only. Columns II, III, IV and V give progressive increase in range at a sacrifice in speed. Manifold pressure (M. P.), gallons per hour (G. P. H.) and true airspeed (T. A. S.) are approximate values for reference. For efficiency maintain indicated airspeed (I. A. S.) hourly. Adjust RPM slightly if necessary to avoid exceeding manifold pressure more than 3 in. Hg.

Range Tables

I — RANGE IN AIR MILES				FUEL U.S. GAL.	II — RANGE IN AIR MILES		III — RANGE IN AIR MILES		IV — RANGE IN AIR MILES		FUEL U.S. GAL.	V — RANGE IN AIR MILES	
STATUTE AT S.L.	STATUTE AT 12,000	NAUTICAL AT S.L.	NAUTICAL AT 12,000		STATUTE	NAUTICAL	STATUTE	NAUTICAL	STATUTE	NAUTICAL		STATUTE	NAUTICAL
				300	50 GAL. ALLOWANCE NOT AVAILABLE IN FLIGHT						300		
410	450	350	390	250	480	420	550	470	610	530	250	710	620
370	410	320	350	225	430	380	490	430	550	470	225	640	560
330	360	280	310	200	390	330	440	380	490	420	200	570	490
290	320	250	270	175	340	290	380	330	430	370	175	500	430
240	270	210	240	150	290	250	330	280	360	320	150	430	370
200	230	180	200	125	240	210	270	240	300	260	125	360	310
160	180	140	160	100	190	170	220	190	240	210	100	280	250
120	140	110	120	75	140	130	160	140	180	160	75	210	190
80	90	70	80	50	100	80	110	90	120	110	50	140	120
40	50	40	40	25	50	40	50	50	60	50	25	70	60

Operating Data

MAXIMUM CONTINUOUS						ALT. Feet	OPERATING DATA (II)						OPERATING DATA (III)					
R.P.M.	I.A.S. M.P.H.	MIXTURE	M.P. In. Hg.	G.P.H.	T.A.S.		R.P.M.	I.A.S. M.P.H.	MIXTURE	M.P. In. Hg.	G.P.H.	T.A.S.	R.P.M.	I.A.S. M.P.H.	MIXTURE	M.P. In. Hg.	G.P.H.	T.A.S.
2600	166	A.R.	44	123	276	30000	2600	166	A.R.	44	123	276						
2600	179	A.R.	44	123	271	25000	2600	179	A.R.	44	123	271						
2600	191	A.R.	44	123	262	20000	2600	191	A.R.	43	123	262	2450	171	A.R.	39	99	240
2600	202	A.R.	44	123	253	15000	2550	197	A.R.	42	116	248	2450	180	A.R.	38	95	231
2600	208	A.R.	44	123	247	12000	2550	201	A.R.	41	112	240	2450	185	A.R.	38	92	224
2600	213	A.R.	44	123	240	9000	2500	203	A.R.	41	108	231	2400	190	A.R.	38	91	219
2600	219	A.R.	44	123	234	6000	2500	207	A.R.	40	105	224	2400	193	A.R.	37	88	212
2600	224	A.R.	44	123	227	3000	2450	209	A.R.	39	101	216	2400	198	A.R.	37	85	206
2600	227	A.R.	44	123	221	S.L.	2450	212	A.R.	39	98	209	2350	199	A.R.	36	82	199

OPERATING DATA (IV)						ALT. Feet	MAXIMUM RANGE (V)					
R.P.M.	I.A.S. M.P.H.	MIXTURE	M.P. In. Hg.	G.P.H.	T.A.S.		R.P.M.	I.A.S. M.P.H.	MIXTURE	M.P. In. Hg.	G.P.H.	T.A.S.
						30000						
						25000						
						20000						
2350	163	A.R.	36	79	212	15000						
2350	168	A.R.	35	77	208	12000						
2350	176	A.R.	35	76	206	9000						
2300	180	A.R.	35	74	200	6000	2100	161	A.L.	34	58	182
2300	185	A.R.	34	72	195	3000	2050	166	A.L.	34	57	179
2300	188	A.R.	34	71	190	S.L.	2050	170	A.L.	33	55	175

Notes

○ ALLOW 50 GAL. FOR TWO ENGINE WARM-UP, TAKE-OFF & INITIAL CLIMB PLUS ALLOWANCE FOR WIND, RESERVE & COMBAT AS REQ'D.

Example

AT 15,700 LB. GROSS WT. WITH 250 GAL. OF FUEL (AFTER DEDUCTING TOTAL ALLOWANCES OF 50 GAL.) TO FLY 600 STAT. AIRMILES AT 12,000 FT. ALT. MAINTAIN 2350 RPM AND 168 MPH IND. AIRSPEED WITH MIXTURE SET A.R.

Legend

I. A. S.: INDICATED AIRSPEED
M. P.: MANIFOLD PRESSURE
G. P. H.: U. S. GAL. PER HOUR
T. A. S.: TRUE AIRSPEED
S. L.: SEA LEVEL

F. T.: FULL THROTTLE
F. R.: FULL RICH
A. R.: AUTO-RICH
A. L.: AUTO-LEAN
C. L.: CRUISING LEAN

FLIGHT OPERATION INSTRUCTION CHART

MODEL(S) P-38J and F-5B

ENGINE(S): V-1710-89 & V-1710-91

EXTERNAL LOAD ITEMS

TANK SUPPORTS ONLY

CHART WEIGHT LIMITS: 17,400 TO 13,500 POUNDS

INSTRUCTIONS FOR USING CHART: Select figure in FUEL column equal to or less than amount of fuel to be used for cruising. Move horizontally to left or right and select RANGE value equal to or greater than the statute or nautical air miles to be flown. Vertically below and opposite desired cruising altitude (ALT.) read optimum R. P. M., I. A. S. and MIXTURE setting required.

NOTES: Column I is for emergency high speed cruising only. Columns II, III, IV and V give progressive increase in range at a sacrifice in speed. Manifold pressure (M. P.), gallons per hour (G. P. H.) and true airspeed (T. A. S.) are approximate values for reference. For efficiency maintain indicated airspeed (I. A. S.) hourly. Adjust RPM slightly if necessary to avoid exceeding manifold pressure more than 3 in. Hg.

LIMITS	R.P.M.	M.P. (IN. HG.)	BLOWER POSITION	MIXTURE POSITION	TIME LIMIT	TOTAL G.P.H.
WAR MAX.	3000	60		AR	5	360
MILITARY POWER	3000	54		AR	15	334
NORMAL RATED	2600	44		AR	NONE	226

I — RANGE IN AIR MILES				FUEL U.S. GAL.	II — RANGE IN AIR MILES		III — RANGE IN AIR MILES		IV — RANGE IN AIR MILES		FUEL U.S. GAL.	V — RANGE IN AIR MILES	
STATUTE		NAUTICAL			STATUTE	NAUTICAL	STATUTE	NAUTICAL	STATUTE	NAUTICAL		STATUTE	NAUTICAL
AT S.L.	AT 12,000	AT S.L.	AT 12,000	410	○ 50 GAL. ALLOWANCE NOT AVAILABLE IN FLIGHT ○						410	1220	1060
400	450	350	390	360	600	520	810	700	1000	870	360	1210	1050
380	430	330	370	340	570	490	760	660	950	820	340	1140	990
350	390	300	340	310	520	450	690	600	870	750	310	1040	910
310	350	270	310	280	470	410	620	540	780	680	280	940	820
280	310	240	270	250	420	360	560	490	700	610	250	840	730
250	280	210	240	220	370	320	490	430	610	530	220	740	640
210	240	180	210	190	320	280	420	370	530	460	190	640	550
180	200	160	170	160	270	230	360	310	450	390	160	540	470
150	160	130	140	130	220	190	290	250	360	310	130	440	380
110	130	100	110	100	170	150	220	190	280	240	100	340	290
80	90	70	80	70	120	100	160	140	200	170	70	240	200

I — MAXIMUM CONTINUOUS						ALT. Feet	II — OPERATING DATA						III — OPERATING DATA						IV — OPERATING DATA						ALT. Feet	V — MAXIMUM RANGE					
R.P.M.	I.A.S. M.P.H.	MIXTURE	M.P. In. Hg.	G.P.H.	T.A.S.		R.P.M.	I.A.S. M.P.H.	MIXTURE	M.P. In. Hg.	G.P.H.	T.A.S.	R.P.M.	I.A.S. M.P.H.	MIXTURE	M.P. In. Hg.	G.P.H.	T.A.S.	R.P.M.	I.A.S. M.P.H.	MIXTURE	M.P. In. Hg.	G.P.H.	T.A.S.		R.P.M.	I.A.S. M.P.H.	MIXTURE	M.P. In. Hg.	G.P.H.	T.A.S.
2600	252	A.R.	44	245	388	30000	2450	240	A.R.	39	200	371	2300	221	A.L.	35	131	346	2050	201	A.L.	32	104	323	30000	1900	172	A.L.	27	77	285
2600	264	A.R.	44	245	374	25000	2450	248	A.R.	38	189	352	2300	232	A.L.	35	131	331	1900	208	A.L.	32	98	304	25000	1750	175	A.L.	27	71	267
2600	277	A.R.	44	245	361	20000	2400	256	A.R.	38	179	335	2250	239	A.L.	34	127	314	1750	212	A.L.	32	91	283	20000	1650	178	A.L.	27	66	248
2600	290	A.R.	44	245	348	15000	2400	267	A.R.	37	172	323	2150	246	A.L.	34	120	298	1650	219	A.L.	33	87	269	15000	1600	178	A.L.	26	61	229
2600	297	A.R.	44	245	340	12000	2350	267	A.R.	36	166	308	2100	249	A.L.	34	116	288	1600	217	A.L.	32	82	255	12000	1600	173	A.L.	25	57	212
2600	302	A.R.	44	245	331	9000	2350	271	A.R.	36	160	298	2050	250	A.L.	33	111	276	1600	217	A.L.	31	78	243	9000	1600	169	A.L.	24	53	199
2600	307	A.R.	44	245	321	6000	2350	273	A.R.	35	154	287	2000	251	A.L.	33	107	265	1600	216	A.L.	30	75	231	6000	1600	165	A.L.	23	50	187
2600	311	A.R.	44	245	311	3000	2300	275	A.R.	35	149	277	1900	251	A.L.	33	102	254	1600	215	A.L.	29	71	221	3000	1600	159	A.L.	22	47	173
2600	314	A.R.	44	245	302	S.L.	2300	279	A.R.	34	144	269	1850	252	A.L.	33	99	245	1600	214	A.L.	28	68	210	S.L	1600	161	A.L.	22	46	168

NOTES

○ ALLOW 50 GAL. FOR WARM-UP, TAKE-OFF & INITIAL CLIMB PLUS ALLOWANCE FOR WIND, RESERVE & COMBAT AS REQ'D.

EXAMPLE

AT 17,400 LB. GROSS WT. WITH 410 GAL. OF FUEL (AFTER DEDUCTING TOTAL ALLOWANCES OF 50 GAL.) TO FLY 1000 STAT. AIRMILES AT 12,000 FT. ALT. MAINTAIN 1600 RPM AND 217 MPH IND. AIRSPEED WITH MIXTURE SET A.L.

LEGEND

I. A. S.: INDICATED AIRSPEED
M. P.: MANIFOLD PRESSURE
G. P. H.: U. S. GAL. PER HOUR
T. A. S.: TRUE AIRSPEED
S. L.: SEA LEVEL
F. T.: FULL THROTTLE
F. R.: FULL RICH
A. R.: AUTO-RICH
A. L.: AUTO-LEAN
C. L.: CRUISING LEAN

MODEL(S)

P-38J and F-5B

ENGINE(S): V-1710-89 & V-1710-91

FLIGHT OPERATION INSTRUCTION CHART

CHART WEIGHT LIMITS: 19,400 TO 14,500 POUNDS

EXTERNAL LOAD ITEMS

TWO 165 GAL. TANKS

LIMITS	R. P. M.	M. P. (IN. HG.)	BLOWER POSITION	MIXTURE POSITION	TIME LIMIT	TOTAL G. P. H.
WAR MAX.	3000	60		AR	5	360
MILITARY POWER	3000	54		AR	15	334
NORMAL RATED	2600	44		AR	NONE	226

INSTRUCTIONS FOR USING CHART: Select figure in FUEL column equal to or less than amount of fuel to be used for cruising. Move horizontally to left or right and select RANGE value equal to or greater than the statute or nautical air miles to be flown. Vertically below and opposite desired cruising altitude (ALT.) read optimum R. P. M., I. A. S. and MIXTURE setting required.

NOTES: Column I is for emergency high speed cruising only. Columns II, III, IV and V give progressive increase in range at a sacrifice in speed. Manifold pressure (M. P.), gallons per hour (G. P. H.) and true airspeed (T. A. S.) are approximate values for reference. For efficiency maintain indicated airspeed (I. A. S.) hourly. Adjust RPM slightly if necessary to avoid exceeding manifold pressure more than 3 in. Hg.

I: Range in air miles, Statute, At S.L.	I: Statute, At 12,000	I: Nautical, At S.L.	I: Nautical, At 12,000	FUEL U.S. GAL.	II: Range in air miles, Statute	II: Nautical	III: Range in air miles, Statute	III: Nautical	IV: Range in air miles, Statute	IV: Nautical	FUEL U.S. GAL.	V: Range in air miles, Statute	V: Nautical
				740	○ 60 GAL. ALLOWANCE NOT AVAILABLE IN FLIGHT ○						740	1780	1560
690	770	590	660	680	950	830	1220	1060	1500	1300	680	1770	1550
640	710	550	620	630	880	770	1130	980	1390	1200	630	1640	1430
580	640	500	560	570	800	700	1030	890	1250	1090	570	1490	1290
520	580	450	500	510	710	620	920	800	1120	970	510	1330	1160
450	510	390	440	450	630	550	810	700	990	860	450	1170	1020
390	440	340	380	390	550	480	700	610	860	740	390	1020	890
330	370	290	320	330	460	400	590	510	730	630	330	860	750
270	310	240	260	270	380	330	490	420	590	520	270	700	610
210	240	180	210	210	290	260	380	330	460	400	210	550	480
150	170	130	150	150	210	180	270	230	330	290	150	390	340
90	100	80	90	90	130	110	160	140	200	170	90	230	200

Maximum Continuous (I), Operating Data (II, III):

Max. Cont. R.P.M.	I.A.S. M.P.H.	MIX-TURE	M.P. In. Hg.	G.P.H.	T.A.S.	ALT. Feet	II R.P.M.	I.A.S. M.P.H.	MIX-TURE	M.P. In. Hg.	G.P.H.	T.A.S.	III R.P.M.	I.A.S. M.P.H.	MIX-TURE	M.P. In. Hg.	G.P.H.	T.A.S.
2600	227	A.R.	44	245	354	30000	2550	221	A.R.	41	223	347	2350	200	A.R.	36	161	322
2600	238	A.R.	44	245	330	25000	2500	229	A.R.	40	210	327	2350	208	A.R.	35	151	304
2600	248	A.R.	44	245	326	20000	2450	234	A.R.	39	198	308	2300	216	A.R.	34	144	287
2600	260	A.R.	44	245	314	15000	2450	242	A.R.	38	189	294	2300	226	A.L.	35	131	276
2600	266	A.R.	44	245	307	12000	2400	246	A.R.	38	183	285	2300	231	A.L.	35	131	268
2600	271	A.R.	44	245	298	9000	2400	249	A.R.	37	175	274	2300	235	A.L.	35	131	261
2600	276	A.R.	44	245	290	6000	2400	251	A.R.	36	169	264	2250	237	A.L.	34	125	251
2600	280	A.R.	44	245	282	3000	2350	253	A.R.	36	164	256	2150	238	A.L.	34	120	241
2600	285	A.R.	44	245	275	S.L.	2350	255	A.R.	36	158	247	2100	239	A.L.	34	115	232

Operating Data (IV), Maximum Range (V):

IV R.P.M.	I.A.S. M.P.H.	MIX-TURE	M.P. In. Hg.	G.P.H.	T.A.S.	ALT. Feet	Max. Range R.P.M.	I.A.S. M.P.H.	MIX-TURE	M.P. In. Hg.	G.P.H.	T.A.S.
2250	190	A.L.	34	126	309	30000	2000	165	A.L.	30	95	276
2150	196	A.L.	34	119	291	25000	1850	170	A.L.	31	89	260
2050	204	A.L.	34	113	275	20000	1700	175	A.L.	31	84	244
2000	210	A.L.	33	107	260	15000	1600	178	A.L.	31	79	229
1900	212	A.L.	33	102	249	12000	1600	176	A.L.	30	74	216
1850	212	A.L.	33	97	239	9000	1600	174	A.L.	29	70	204
1800	213	A.L.	33	94	229	6000	1600	171	A.L.	28	66	192
1700	213	A.L.	33	90	219	3000	1600	169	A.L.	27	62	181
1650	213	A.L.	32	86	210	S.L.	1600	163	A.L.	26	58	169

NOTES

○ ALLOW 60 GAL. FOR WARM-UP, TAKE-OFF & INITIAL CLIMB PLUS ALLOWANCE FOR WIND, RESERVE & COMBAT AS REQ'D.

EXAMPLE

AT 19,400 LB. GROSS WT. WITH 740 GAL. OF FUEL (AFTER DEDUCTING TOTAL ALLOWANCES OF 60 GAL.) TO FLY 1500 STAT. AIRMILES AT 12,000 FT. ALT. MAINTAIN 1900 RPM AND 212 MPH IND. AIRSPEED WITH MIXTURE SET A.L.

LEGEND

I. A. S.: INDICATED AIRSPEED
M. P.: MANIFOLD PRESSURE
G. P. H.: U. S. GAL. PER HOUR
T. A. S.: TRUE AIRSPEED
S. L.: SEA LEVEL
F. T.: FULL THROTTLE
F. R.: FULL RICH
A. R.: AUTO-RICH
A. L.: AUTO-LEAN
C. L.: CRUISING LEAN

FLIGHT OPERATION INSTRUCTION CHART

MODEL(S)

P—38J and F—5B

ENGINE(S): V-1710-89 & V-1710-91

CHART WEIGHT LIMITS: 21,400 TO 14,500 POUNDS

EXTERNAL LOAD ITEMS

TWO 300 GALLON TANKS

LIMITS	R.P.M.	M.P. (IN. HG.)	BLOWER POSITION	MIXTURE POSITION	TIME LIMIT	TOTAL G.P.H.
WAR MAX.	3000	60		AR	5	360
MILITARY POWER	3000	54		AR	15	334
NORMAL RATED	2600	44		AR	NONE	226

INSTRUCTIONS FOR USING CHART: Select figure in FUEL column equal to or less than amount of fuel to be used for cruising. Move horizontally to left or right and select RANGE value equal to or greater than the statute or nautical air miles to be flown. Vertically below and opposite desired cruising altitude (ALT.) read optimum R. P. M., I. A. S. and MIXTURE setting required.

NOTES: Column I is for emergency high speed cruising only. Columns II, III, IV and V give progressive increase in range at a sacrifice in speed. Manifold pressure (M. P.), gallons per hour (G. P. H.) and true airspeed (T. A. S.) are approximate values for reference. For efficiency maintain indicated airspeed (I. A. S.) hourly. Adjust RPM slightly if necessary to avoid exceeding manifold pressure more than 3 in. Hg.

I RANGE IN AIR MILES		FUEL U.S. GAL.	II RANGE IN AIR MILES		III RANGE IN AIR MILES		IV RANGE IN AIR MILES		FUEL U.S. GAL.	V RANGE IN AIR MILES	
STATUTE	NAUTICAL		STATUTE	NAUTICAL	STATUTE	NAUTICAL	STATUTE	NAUTICAL		STATUTE	NAUTICAL
		1010	○ 60 GAL. ALLOWANCE NOT AVAILABLE IN FLIGHT ○						1010	2210	1930
		1010	1240	1080	1560	1350	1870	1630	950	2200	1920
		920	1210	1050	1510	1310	1810	1570	920	2130	1860
		830	1090	950	1360	1180	1640	1420	830	1930	1680
		740	970	840	1210	1050	1460	1270	740	1720	1490
Use Column 2		650	850	740	1070	920	1280	1110	650	1510	1310
		560	730	640	920	800	1100	960	560	1300	1130
		470	620	540	770	670	930	800	470	1090	950
		380	500	430	620	540	750	650	380	880	770
		290	380	330	480	410	570	500	290	670	590
		200	260	230	330	280	390	340	200	460	400
		110	140	130	180	160	220	190	110	260	220

MAXIMUM CONTINUOUS

R.P.M.	I.A.S. M.P.H.	MIXTURE	M.P. In. Hg.	G.P.H.	T.A.S.	ALT. Feet	R.P.M.	I.A.S. M.P.H.	MIXTURE	M.P. In. Hg.	G.P.H.	T.A.S.	R.P.M.	I.A.S. M.P.H.	MIXTURE	M.P. In. Hg.	G.P.H.	T.A.S.	R.P.M.	I.A.S. M.P.H.	MIXTURE	M.P. In. Hg.	G.P.H.	T.A.S.	ALT. Feet	R.P.M.	I.A.S. M.P.H.	MIXTURE	M.P. In. Hg.	G.P.H.	T.A.S.
									OPERATING DATA						OPERATING DATA						OPERATING DATA						MAXIMUM RANGE				
						30000	2550	214	A.R.	42	232	338	2400	194	A.R.	37	172	314	2300	181	A.L.	35	131	298	30000	2050	158	A.L.	32	104	267
						25000	2550	221	A.R.	41	219	319	2350	201	A.R.	36	162	296	2300	192	A.L.	35	131	287	25000	1900	167	A.L.	32	98	254
Use Column 2						20000	2500	230	A.R.	40	207	302	2350	210	A.R.	35	154	282	2200	200	A.L.	34	124	272	20000	1750	174	A.L.	33	94	243
						15000	2450	237	A.R.	39	197	288	2300	219	A.R.	35	148	269	2150	207	A.L.	34	117	257	15000	1700	178	A.L.	33	88	229
						12000	2450	239	A.R.	38	190	278	2300	222	A.R.	34	143	259	2050	209	A.L.	34	113	247	12000	1600	178	A.L.	33	85	218
Max. Permissible IAS with						9000	2450	242	A.R.	38	184	269	2300	226	A.L.	35	131	251	2000	211	A.L.	33	108	238	9000	1600	178	A.L.	32	80	208
300 gallon tanks- 250 MPH.						6000	2400	245	A.R.	37	178	260	2300	231	A.L.	35	131	245	1950	212	A.L.	33	104	228	6000	1600	175	A.L.	30	76	196
						3000	2400	247	A.R.	37	171	250	2300	236	A.L.	35	131	239	1850	213	A.L.	33	99	218	3000	1600	172	A.L.	29	71	185
						S.L.	2350	250	A.R.	36	166	242	2250	238	A.L.	34	127	231	1800	214	A.L.	33	96	211	S.L.	1600	162	A.L.	28	65	168

NOTES

○ ALLOW 60 GAL. FOR WARM-UP, TAKE-OFF & INITIAL CLIMB PLUS ALLOWANCE FOR WIND, RESERVE & COMBAT AS REQ'D.

EXAMPLE

AT 21,400 LB. GROSS WT. WITH 1010 GAL. OF FUEL (AFTER DEDUCTING TOTAL ALLOWANCES OF 60 GAL.) TO FLY 1860 STAT. AIRMILES AT 12,000 FT. ALT. MAINTAIN 2050 RPM AND 209 MPH IND. AIRSPEED WITH MIXTURE SET A.L.

LEGEND

I. A. S.: INDICATED AIRSPEED
M. P.: MANIFOLD PRESSURE
G. P. H.: U. S. GAL. PER HOUR
T. A. S.: TRUE AIRSPEED
S. L.: SEA LEVEL

F. T.: FULL THROTTLE
F. R.: FULL RICH
A. R.: AUTO-RICH
A. L.: AUTO-LEAN
C. L.: CRUISING LEAN

RED FIGURES ARE PRELIMINARY, SUBJECT TO REVISION AFTER FLIGHT CHECK

MODEL(S)

P-38J and F-5B
SINGLE ENGINE OPERATION
ENGINE(S): V-1710-89 & V-1710-91

FLIGHT OPERATION INSTRUCTION CHART

CHART WEIGHT LIMITS: 17,000 TO 13,500 POUNDS

EXTERNAL LOAD ITEMS
SINGLE ENGINE OPERATION
DEAD PROPELLER FEATHERED
EXTERNAL TANK SUPPORTS ONLY

LIMITS	R.P.M.	M.P. (IN. HG.)	BLOWER POSITION	MIXTURE POSITION	TIME LIMIT	TOTAL G.P.H.
WAR MAX.	3000	60		AR	5	360
MILITARY POWER	3000	54		AR	15	334
NORMAL RATED	2600	44		AR	NONE	226

INSTRUCTIONS FOR USING CHART: Select figure in FUEL column equal to or less than amount of fuel to be used for cruising. Move horizontally to left or right and select RANGE value equal to or greater than the statute or nautical air miles to be flown. Vertically below and opposite desired cruising altitude (ALT.) read optimum R. P. M., I. A. S. and MIXTURE setting required.

NOTES: Column I is for emergency high speed cruising only. Columns II, III, IV and V give progressive increase in range at a sacrifice in speed. Manifold pressure (M. P.), gallons per hour (G. P. H.) and true airspeed (T. A. S.) are approximate values for reference. For efficiency maintain indicated airspeed (I. A. S.) hourly. Adjust RPM slightly if necessary to avoid exceeding manifold pressure more than 3 in. Hg.

Range in Air Miles

I — STATUTE (AT S.L.)	I — STATUTE (AT 12,000)	I — NAUTICAL (AT S.L.)	I — NAUTICAL (AT 12,000)	FUEL U.S. GAL.	II — STATUTE	II — NAUTICAL	III — STATUTE	III — NAUTICAL	IV — STATUTE	IV — NAUTICAL	FUEL U.S. GAL.	V — STATUTE	V — NAUTICAL
				410	50 GAL. ALLOWANCE NOT AVAILABLE IN FLIGHT						410		
580	630	500	550	360	680	590	750	650	840	730	360	930	810
530	580	460	500	330	620	540	690	600	770	670	330	850	740
480	530	420	460	300	570	490	630	540	700	610	300	770	670
430	480	380	410	270	510	440	560	490	630	550	270	690	600
380	420	330	370	240	450	390	500	430	560	480	240	620	540
340	370	290	320	210	400	340	440	380	490	420	210	540	470
290	320	250	280	180	340	300	380	330	420	360	180	460	400
240	260	210	230	150	280	250	310	270	350	300	150	390	340
190	210	170	180	120	230	200	250	220	280	240	120	310	270
140	160	130	140	90	170	150	190	160	210	180	90	230	200

Operating Data

MAXIMUM CONTINUOUS R.P.M.	I.A.S. M.P.H.	MIX-TURE	M.P. In. Hg.	G.P.H.	T.A.S.	ALT. Feet	II R.P.M.	I.A.S. M.P.H.	MIX-TURE	M.P. In. Hg.	G.P.H.	T.A.S.	III R.P.M.	I.A.S. M.P.H.	MIX-TURE	M.P. In. Hg.	G.P.H.	T.A.S.	IV R.P.M.	I.A.S. M.P.H.	MIX-TURE	M.P. In. Hg.	G.P.H.	T.A.S.	ALT. Feet	MAXIMUM RANGE R.P.M.	I.A.S. M.P.H.	MIX-TURE	M.P. In. Hg.	G.P.H.	T.A.S.
2600	151	A.R.	44	123	257	30000																			30000						
2600	167	A.R.	44	123	256	25000	2600	167	A.R.	43	121	254													25000						
2600	187	A.R.	44	123	252	20000	2550	178	A.R.	43	118	247	2450	152	A.R.	38	93	217							20000						
2600	195	A.R.	44	123	245	15000	2550	187	A.R.	42	113	238	2450	169	A.R.	38	94	219							15000						
2600	202	A.R.	44	123	241	12000	2550	191	A.R.	41	110	230	2450	174	A.R.	38	92	214	2300	149	A.R.	34	72	188	12000						
2600	208	A.R.	44	123	235	9000	2500	196	A.R.	40	107	224	2400	180	A.R.	38	90	210	2300	160	A.R.	35	74	191	9000	2300	156	A.L.	35	65	187
2600	214	A.R.	44	123	230	6000	2500	200	A.R.	40	104	218	2400	186	A.R.	37	89	205	2300	167	A.R.	34	73	188	6000	2250	161	A.L.	34	64	183
2600	220	A.R.	44	123	224	3000	2450	204	A.R.	39	101	211	2400	190	A.R.	37	86	200	2300	173	A.R.	34	71	185	3000	2250	167	A.L.	34	63	180
2600	223	A.R.	44	123	218	S.L.	2450	207	A.R.	39	97	205	2400	195	A.R.	36	84	195	2300	179	A.R.	34	70	183	S.L.	2200	173	A.L.	34	62	178

NOTES

ALLOW 50 GAL. FOR TWO ENGINE WARM-UP, TAKE-OFF & INITIAL CLIMB PLUS ALLOWANCE FOR WIND, RESERVE & COMBAT AS REQ'D.

EXAMPLE

AT 17,000 LB. GROSS WT. WITH 360 GAL. OF FUEL (AFTER DEDUCTING TOTAL ALLOWANCES OF 50 GAL.) TO FLY 800 STAT. AIRMILES AT 12,000 FT. ALT. MAINTAIN 2300 RPM AND 149 MPH IND. AIRSPEED WITH MIXTURE SET A.L.

LEGEND

I. A. S.: INDICATED AIRSPEED
M. P.: MANIFOLD PRESSURE
G. P. H.: U. S. GAL. PER HOUR
T. A. S.: TRUE AIRSPEED
S. L.: SEA LEVEL
F. T.: FULL THROTTLE
F. R.: FULL RICH
A. R.: AUTO-RICH
A. L.: AUTO-LEAN
C. L.: CRUISING LEAN

RED FIGURES ARE PRELIMINARY, SUBJECT TO REVISION AFTER FLIGHT CHECK

FLIGHT OPERATION INSTRUCTION CHART

MODEL(S): P-38L

ENGINE(S): V-1710-111 & V-1710-113

EXTERNAL LOAD ITEMS — TANK SUPPORTS ONLY

CHART WEIGHT LIMITS: 17,400 TO 13,500 POUNDS

LIMITS	R.P.M.	M.P. (IN. HG.)	BLOWER POSITION	MIXTURE POSITION	TIME LIMIT	TOTAL G.P.H.
WAR MAX.	3000	60		AR	5	360
MILITARY POWER	3000	54		AR	15	334
NORMAL RATED	2600	44		AR	NONE	226

INSTRUCTIONS FOR USING CHART: Select figure in FUEL column equal to or less than amount of fuel to be used for cruising. Move horizontally to left or right and select RANGE value equal to or greater than the statute or nautical air miles to be flown. Vertically below and opposite desired cruising altitude (ALT.) read optimum R. P. M., I. A. S. and MIXTURE setting required.

NOTES: Column I is for emergency high speed cruising only. Columns II, III, IV and V give progressive increase in range at a sacrifice in speed. Manifold pressure (M. P.), gallons per hour (G. P. H.) and true airspeed (T. A. S.) are approximate values for reference. For efficiency maintain indicated airspeed (I. A. S.) hourly. Adjust RPM slightly if necessary to avoid exceeding manifold pressure more than 3 in. Hg.

Range in Air Miles

	I STATUTE AT S.L.	I STATUTE AT 12,000	I NAUTICAL AT S.L.	I NAUTICAL AT 12,000	FUEL U.S. GAL.	II STATUTE	II NAUTICAL	III STATUTE	III NAUTICAL	IV STATUTE	IV NAUTICAL	FUEL U.S. GAL.	V STATUTE	V NAUTICAL
					410	○ 50 GAL. ALLOWANCE NOT AVAILABLE IN FLIGHT ○						410		
	400	450	350	390	360	600	520	810	700	1000	870	360	1210	1050
	380	430	330	370	340	570	490	760	660	950	820	340	1140	990
	350	390	300	340	310	520	450	690	600	870	750	310	1040	910
	310	350	270	310	280	470	410	620	540	780	680	280	940	820
	280	310	240	270	250	420	360	560	490	700	610	250	840	730
	250	280	210	240	220	370	320	490	430	610	530	220	740	640
	210	240	180	210	190	320	280	420	370	530	460	190	640	550
	180	200	160	170	160	270	230	360	310	450	390	160	540	470
	150	160	130	140	130	220	190	290	250	360	310	130	440	380
	110	130	100	110	100	170	150	220	190	280	240	100	340	290
	80	90	70	80	70	120	100	160	140	200	170	70	240	200

Operating Data

I — MAXIMUM CONTINUOUS

R.P.M.	I.A.S. M.P.H.	MIXTURE	M.P. In. Hg.	G.P.H.	T.A.S.	ALT. Feet
2600	252	A.R.	44	245	388	30000
2600	264	A.R.	44	245	374	25000
2600	277	A.R.	44	245	361	20000
2600	290	A.R.	44	245	348	15000
2600	297	A.R.	44	245	340	12000
2600	302	A.R.	44	245	331	9000
2600	307	A.R.	44	245	321	6000
2600	311	A.R.	44	245	311	3000
2600	314	A.R.	44	245	302	S.L.

II — OPERATING DATA

R.P.M.	I.A.S. M.P.H.	MIXTURE	M.P. In. Hg.	G.P.H.	T.A.S.
2450	240	A.R.	39	200	371
2450	248	A.R.	38	189	352
2450	256	A.R.	38	179	335
2400	267	A.R.	37	172	323
2350	267	A.R.	36	166	308
2350	271	A.R.	36	160	298
2350	273	A.R.	35	154	287
2300	275	A.R.	35	149	277
2300	279	A.R.	34	144	269

III — OPERATING DATA

R.P.M.	I.A.S. M.P.H.	MIXTURE	M.P. In. Hg.	G.P.H.	T.A.S.
2300	221	A.L.	35	131	346
2300	232	A.L.	35	131	331
2250	239	A.L.	34	127	314
2150	246	A.L.	34	120	298
2100	249	A.L.	34	116	288
2050	250	A.L.	33	111	276
2000	251	A.L.	33	107	265
1900	251	A.L.	33	102	254
1850	252	A.L.	33	99	245

IV — OPERATING DATA

R.P.M.	I.A.S. M.P.H.	MIXTURE	M.P. In. Hg.	G.P.H.	T.A.S.	ALT. Feet
2050	201	A.L.	32	104	323	30000
1900	208	A.L.	32	98	304	25000
1750	212	A.L.	32	91	283	20000
1650	219	A.L.	33	87	269	15000
1600	217	A.L.	32	82	255	12000
1600	217	A.L.	31	78	243	9000
1600	216	A.L.	30	75	231	6000
1600	215	A.L.	29	71	221	3000
1600	214	A.L.	28	68	210	S.L.

V — MAXIMUM RANGE

R.P.M.	I.A.S. M.P.H.	MIXTURE	M.P. In. Hg.	G.P.H.	T.A.S.
1900	172	A.L.	27	77	285
1750	175	A.L.	27	71	267
1650	178	A.L.	27	66	248
1600	178	A.L.	26	61	229
1600	173	A.L.	25	57	212
1600	169	A.L.	24	53	199
1600	165	A.L.	23	50	187
1600	159	A.L.	22	47	173
1600	161	A.L.	22	46	168

NOTES

○ ALLOW 50 GAL. FOR WARM-UP, TAKE-OFF & INITIAL CLIMB PLUS ALLOWANCE FOR WIND, RESERVE & COMBAT AS REQ'D.

EXAMPLE

AT 17,400 LB. GROSS WT. WITH 410 GAL. OF FUEL (AFTER DEDUCTING TOTAL ALLOWANCES OF 50 GAL.) TO FLY 1000 STAT. AIRMILES AT 12,000 FT. ALT. MAINTAIN 1600 RPM AND 217 MPH IND. AIRSPEED WITH MIXTURE SET A.L.

LEGEND

I. A. S.: INDICATED AIRSPEED
M. P.: MANIFOLD PRESSURE
G. P. H.: U. S. GAL. PER HOUR
T. A. S.: TRUE AIRSPEED
S. L.: SEA LEVEL
F. T.: FULL THROTTLE
F. R.: FULL RICH
A. R.: AUTO-RICH
A. L.: AUTO-LEAN
C. L.: CRUISING LEAN

RED FIGURES ARE PRELIMINARY, SUBJECT TO REVISION AFTER FLIGHT CHECK

FLIGHT OPERATION INSTRUCTION CHART

MODEL(S) P-38L

EXTERNAL LOAD ITEMS — TWO 165 GALLON TANKS

ENGINE(S): V-1710-111 & V-1710-113

CHART WEIGHT LIMITS: 19,400 TO 14,500 POUNDS

LIMITS	R.P.M.	M.P. (IN. HG.)	BLOWER POSITION	MIXTURE POSITION	TIME LIMIT	TOTAL G.P.H.
WAR MAX.	3000	60		AR	5	360
MILITARY POWER	3000	54		AR	15	334
NORMAL RATED	2600	44		AR	NONE.	226

INSTRUCTIONS FOR USING CHART: Select figure in FUEL column equal to or less than amount of fuel to be used for cruising. Move horizontally to left or right and select RANGE value equal to or greater than the statute or nautical air miles to be flown. Vertically below and opposite desired cruising altitude (ALT.) read optimum R. P. M., I. A. S. and MIXTURE setting required.

NOTES: Column I is for emergency high speed cruising only. Columns II, III, IV and V give progressive increase in range at a sacrifice in speed. Manifold pressure (M. P.), gallons per hour (G. P. H.) and true airspeed (T. A. S.) are approximate values for reference. For efficiency maintain indicated airspeed (I. A. S.) hourly. Adjust RPM slightly if necessary to avoid exceeding manifold pressure more than 3 in. Hg.

RANGE IN AIR MILES

I STATUTE AT S.L.	I STATUTE AT 12,000	I NAUTICAL AT S.L.	I NAUTICAL AT 12,000	FUEL U.S. GAL.	II STATUTE	II NAUTICAL	III STATUTE	III NAUTICAL	IV STATUTE	IV NAUTICAL	FUEL U.S. GAL.	V STATUTE	V NAUTICAL
				740	○ 60 GAL. ALLOWANCE NOT AVAILABLE IN FLIGHT ○						740		
690	770	590	660	680	950	830	1220	1060	1500	1300	680	1770	1550
640	710	550	620	630	880	770	1130	980	1390	1200	630	1640	1430
580	640	500	560	570	800	700	1030	890	1250	1090	570	1490	1290
520	580	450	500	510	710	620	920	800	1120	970	510	1330	1160
450	510	390	440	450	630	550	810	700	990	860	450	1170	1020
390	440	340	380	390	550	480	700	610	860	740	390	1020	890
330	370	290	320	330	460	400	590	510	730	630	330	860	750
270	310	240	260	270	380	330	490	420	590	520	270	700	610
210	240	180	210	210	290	260	380	330	460	400	210	550	480
150	170	130	150	150	210	180	270	230	330	290	150	390	340
90	100	80	90	90	130	110	160	140	200	170	90	230	200

OPERATING DATA

I MAXIMUM CONTINUOUS R.P.M.	I I.A.S. M.P.H.	I MIXTURE	I M.P. In. Hg.	I G.P.H.	I T.A.S.	ALT. Feet	II R.P.M.	II I.A.S. M.P.H.	II MIXTURE	II M.P. In. Hg.	II G.P.H.	II T.A.S.	III R.P.M.	III I.A.S. M.P.H.	III MIXTURE	III M.P. In. Hg.	III G.P.H.	III T.A.S.	IV R.P.M.	IV I.A.S. M.P.H.	IV MIXTURE	IV M.P. In. Hg.	IV G.P.H.	IV T.A.S.	ALT. Feet	V MAXIMUM RANGE R.P.M.	V I.A.S. M.P.H.	V MIXTURE	V M.P. In. Hg.	V G.P.H.	V T.A.S.
2600	227	A.R.	44	245	354	30000	2550	221	A.R.	41	223	347	2350	200	A.R.	36	161	322	2250	190	A.L.	34	126	309	30000	2000	165	A.L.	30	95	276
2600	238	A.R.	44	245	330	25000	2500	229	A.R.	40	210	327	2350	208	A.R.	35	151	304	2150	196	A.L.	34	119	291	25000	1850	170	A.L.	31	89	260
2600	248	A.R.	44	245	326	20000	2450	234	A.R.	39	198	308	2300	216	A.R.	34	144	287	2050	204	A.L.	34	113	275	20000	1700	175	A.L.	31	84	244
2600	260	A.R.	44	245	314	15000	2450	242	A.R.	38	189	294	2300	226	A.L.	35	131	276	2000	210	A.L.	33	107	260	15000	1600	178	A.L.	31	79	229
2600	266	A.R.	44	245	307	12000	2400	246	A.R.	38	183	285	2300	231	A.L.	35	131	268	1900	212	A.L.	33	102	249	12000	1600	176	A.L.	30	74	216
2600	271	A.R.	44	245	298	9000	2400	249	A.R.	37	175	274	2300	235	A.L.	35	131	261	1850	212	A.L.	33	97	239	9000	1600	174	A.L.	29	70	204
2600	276	A.R.	44	245	290	6000	2400	251	A.R.	36	169	264	2250	237	A.L.	34	125	251	1800	213	A.L.	33	94	229	6000	1600	171	A.L.	28	66	192
2600	280	A.R.	44	245	282	3000	2350	253	A.R.	36	164	256	2150	238	A.L.	34	120	241	1700	213	A.L.	33	90	219	3000	1600	169	A.L.	27	62	181
2600	285	A.R.	44	245	275	S.L.	2350	255	A.R.	36	158	247	2100	239	A.L.	34	115	232	1650	213	A.L.	32	86	210	S.L.	1600	163	A.L.	26	58	169

NOTES

○ ALLOW 60 GAL. FOR WARM-UP, TAKE-OFF & INITIAL CLIMB PLUS ALLOWANCE FOR WIND, RESERVE & COMBAT AS REQ'D.

EXAMPLE

AT 19,400 LB. GROSS WT. WITH 740 GAL. OF FUEL (AFTER DEDUCTING TOTAL ALLOWANCES OF 60 GAL.) TO FLY 1500 STAT. AIRMILES AT 12,000 FT. ALT. MAINTAIN 1900 RPM AND 212 MPH IND. AIRSPEED WITH MIXTURE SET A.L.

LEGEND

I. A. S.: INDICATED AIRSPEED
M. P.: MANIFOLD PRESSURE
G. P. H.: U. S. GAL. PER HOUR
T. A. S.: TRUE AIRSPEED
S. L.: SEA LEVEL
F. T.: FULL THROTTLE
F. R.: FULL RICH
A. R.: AUTO-RICH
A. L.: AUTO-LEAN
C. L.: CRUISING LEAN

RED FIGURES ARE PRELIMINARY, SUBJECT TO REVISION AFTER FLIGHT CHECK

FLIGHT OPERATION INSTRUCTION CHART

MODEL(S) P-38 L

ENGINE(S): V-1710-111 & V-1710-113

CHART WEIGHT LIMITS: 21,400 TO 14,500 POUNDS

EXTERNAL LOAD ITEMS

TWO 300 GALLON TANKS

LIMITS	R.P.M.	M.P. (IN. HG.)	BLOWER POSITION	MIXTURE POSITION	TIME LIMIT	TOTAL G.P.H.
WAR MAX.	3000	60		AR	5	360
MILITARY POWER	3000	54		AR	15	334
NORMAL RATED	2600	44		AR	NONE	226

INSTRUCTIONS FOR USING CHART: Select figure in FUEL column equal to or less than amount of fuel to be used for cruising. Move horizontally to left or right and select RANGE value equal to or greater than the statute or nautical air miles to be flown. Vertically below and opposite desired cruising altitude (ALT.) read optimum R. P. M., I. A. S. and MIXTURE setting required.

NOTES: Column I is for emergency high speed cruising only. Columns II, III, IV and V give progressive increase in range at a sacrifice in speed. Manifold pressure (M. P.), gallons per hour (G. P. H.) and true airspeed (T. A. S.) are approximate values for reference. For efficiency maintain indicated airspeed (I. A. S.) hourly. Adjust RPM slightly if necessary to avoid exceeding manifold pressure more than 3 in. Hg.

I — RANGE IN AIR MILES		FUEL U.S. GAL.	II — RANGE IN AIR MILES		III — RANGE IN AIR MILES		IV — RANGE IN AIR MILES		FUEL U.S. GAL.	V — RANGE IN AIR MILES	
STATUTE	NAUTICAL		STATUTE	NAUTICAL	STATUTE	NAUTICAL	STATUTE	NAUTICAL		STATUTE	NAUTICAL
		1010	◯ 60 GAL. ALLOWANCE NOT AVAILABLE IN FLIGHT ◯						1010		
		950	1240	1080	1560	1350	1870	1630	950	2200	1920
		920	1210	1050	1510	1310	1810	1570	920	2130	1860
		830	1090	950	1360	1180	1640	1420	830	1930	1680
Use Column 2		740	970	840	1210	1050	1460	1270	740	1720	1490
		650	850	740	1070	920	1280	1110	650	1510	1310
		560	730	640	920	800	1100	960	560	1300	1130
		470	620	540	770	670	930	800	470	1090	950
		380	500	430	620	540	750	650	380	880	770
		290	380	330	480	410	570	500	290	670	590
		200	260	230	330	280	390	340	200	460	400
		110	140	130	180	160	220	190	110	260	220

MAXIMUM CONTINUOUS (R.P.M. | I.A.S. M.P.H. | MIXTURE | M.P. In. Hg. | G.P.H. | T.A.S.): Use Column 2. Max. Permissible IAS with 300 gallon tanks—250 MPH.

ALT. Feet	II R.P.M.	I.A.S.	MIX.	M.P.	G.P.H.	T.A.S.	III R.P.M.	I.A.S.	MIX.	M.P.	G.P.H.	T.A.S.	IV R.P.M.	I.A.S.	MIX.	M.P.	G.P.H.	T.A.S.	ALT. Feet	V R.P.M.	I.A.S.	MIX.	M.P.	G.P.H.	T.A.S.
30000	2550	214	A.R.	42	232	338	2400	194	A.R.	37	172	314	2300	181	A.L.	35	131	298	30000	2050	158	A.L.	32	104	267
25000	2550	221	A.R.	41	219	319	2350	201	A.R.	36	162	296	2300	192	A.L.	35	131	287	25000	1900	167	A.L.	32	98	254
20000	2500	230	A.R.	40	207	302	2350	210	A.R.	35	154	282	2200	200	A.L.	34	124	272	20000	1750	174	A.L.	33	94	243
15000	2450	237	A.R.	39	197	288	2300	219	A.R.	35	148	269	2150	207	A.L.	34	117	257	15000	1700	178	A.L.	33	88	229
12000	2450	239	A.R.	38	190	278	2300	222	A.R.	34	143	259	2050	209	A.L.	34	113	247	12000	1600	178	A.L.	33	85	218
9000	2450	242	A.R.	38	184	269	2300	226	A.L.	35	131	251	2000	211	A.L.	33	108	238	9000	1600	178	A.L.	32	80	208
6000	2400	245	A.R.	37	178	260	2300	231	A.L.	35	131	245	1950	212	A.L.	33	104	228	6000	1600	175	A.L.	30	76	196
3000	2400	247	A.R.	37	171	250	2300	236	A.L.	35	131	239	1850	213	A.L.	33	99	218	3000	1600	172	A.L.	29	71	185
S.L.	2350	250	A.R.	36	166	242	2250	238	A.L.	34	127	231	1800	214	A.L.	33	96	211	S.L.	1600	162	A.L.	28	65	168

NOTES

◯ ALLOW 60 GAL. FOR WARM-UP, TAKE-OFF & INITIAL CLIMB PLUS ALLOWANCE FOR WIND, RESERVE & COMBAT AS REQ'D.

EXAMPLE

AT 21,400 LB. GROSS WT. WITH 1010 GAL. OF FUEL (AFTER DEDUCTING TOTAL ALLOWANCES OF 60 GAL.) TO FLY 1860 STAT. AIRMILES AT 12,000 FT. ALT. MAINTAIN 2050 RPM AND 209 MPH IND. AIRSPEED WITH MIXTURE SET A.L.

LEGEND

I. A. S.: INDICATED AIRSPEED
M. P.: MANIFOLD PRESSURE
G. P. H.: U. S. GAL. PER HOUR
T. A. S.: TRUE AIRSPEED
S. L.: SEA LEVEL
F. T.: FULL THROTTLE
F. R.: FULL RICH
A. R.: AUTO-RICH
A. L.: AUTO-LEAN
C. L.: CRUISING LEAN

RED FIGURES ARE PRELIMINARY, SUBJECT TO REVISION AFTER FLIGHT CHECK